Contents

Edited by **Sally Smith**

5	**Sheep and shepherds** Fiona Stratta	
20	**St Benedict** John Fitzmaurice	*15–28 May*
33	**The prodigal** Janet Fletcher	*29 May–11 June*
47	**Esther** Andrea Skevington	*12–25 June*
60	**Peter** Sally Smith	*26 June–9 July*
72	**Walls and boundaries** Janet Lunt	*10–23 July*
87	**Beside the sea** Dorinda Miller	*24 July–6 August*
101	**The wisdom of God in creation** Lisa Cherrett	*7–20 August*
114	**Listening** Liz Hoare	*21 August–3 September*
127	**On holiday with God** Sally Smith	
130	**As a Child: Obedient** Phil Steer	
136	**Spotlight: The Greenhouse Christian Centre** Kate Strand	

The Bible Reading Fellowship
15 The Chambers, Vineyard
Abingdon OX14 3FE
brf.org.uk

The Bible Reading Fellowship (BRF) is a Registered Charity (233280)

ISBN 978 0 85746 454 5
All rights reserved

This edition © The Bible Reading Fellowship 2017

Cover image © Benjamin Statham

Acknowledgements
Unless otherwise stated, scripture quotations are taken from The Holy Bible, New International Version (Anglicised edition) copyright © 1973, 1978, 1984, 2011 by Biblica, used by permission of Hodder & Stoughton Publishers, an Hachette UK company. All rights reserved. 'NIV' is a registered trade mark of Biblica (formerly International Bible Society). UK trademark number 1448790.

Scripture quotations taken from The Holy Bible, New International Version, copyright © 1973, 1978, 1984 by International Bible Society, are used by permission of Hodder & Stoughton, a member of the Hachette Livre UK Group. All rights reserved. 'NIV' is a registered trademark of International Bible Society. UK trademark number 1448790.

Scripture quotations taken from The New Revised Standard Version of the Bible, Anglicised Edition, copyright © 1989, 1995 by the Division of Christian Education of the National Council of the Churches of Christ in the USA, are used by permission. All rights reserved.

Scripture quotations taken from the Holy Bible, New Living Translation, copyright © 1996, 2004, 2007, 2013. Used by permission of Tyndale House Publishers, Inc., Carol Stream, Illinois 60188. All rights reserved.

Scripture quotations taken from the Holy Bible, English Standard Version, published by HarperCollins Publishers, © 2001 Crossway Bibles, a division of Good News Publishers. Used by permission. All rights reserved.

Scripture taken from *The Message*. Copyright © 1993, 1994, 1995, 1996, 2000, 2001, 2002. Used by permission of NavPress Publishing Group.

Extract from *As a Child* by Phil Steer, published by lulu.com, 2012.

Every effort has been made to trace and contact copyright owners for material used in this resource. We apologise for any inadvertent omissions or errors, and would ask those concerned to contact us so that full acknowledgement can be made in the future.

Printed by Gutenberg Press, Tarxien, Malta

Sally Smith writes...

Welcome to this issue of *Quiet Spaces*.

Some ways of praying occur more than once in each issue of *Quiet Spaces*. In this issue the traditional practice of *lectio divina* is used twice. You will find that each writer describes the practice in a slightly different way. They may take a different approach to match the material they are exploring, or they may have different personal approaches, which they are reflecting. As with all the exercises in *Quiet Spaces*, do feel free to use the approach that best suits you. You may find that you develop your own version of *lectio divina*, or any of the other practices used, that enables you to use the passage to pray. Try not to get too lost in the mechanics of the practice, but allow God to lead you through, so that it becomes a natural process for you. You are aiming to receive a small part of the passage as a gift from God, and then to cherish that gift and allow it to move from your head to the deeper places where God loves to meet you. Allow God to use the words, but also be ready to move beyond the words as you meet and receive from him.

I know from readers who have been in touch, and from those I have met, that many of you are using *Quiet Spaces* in your own individual way, and that you appreciate the freedom to use what enables you to encounter God and to leave sections which you believe may not be as helpful. I would challenge you sometimes to be adventurous and to try some new ways of praying—you may find that you are pleasantly surprised and begin to experience God in new ways. He delights in leading us along new paths to new pastures when we dare to listen and follow him.

So, have a prayerful summer and do get in touch to let us know how you get on in your adventures.

Writers in this issue

Fiona Stratta is a Speech and Language therapist and Speech and Drama teacher. She has written *Walking with Gospel Women* and *Walking with Old Testament Women* for BRF, with *Walking with Biblical Women of Courage* published in July 2017. In her writing she desires to connect readers' spiritual journeys more closely with their daily lives.

John Fitzmaurice is Director of Ordinands and Vocation in the Diocese of Worcester. He has a master's degree in the psychology of religion and a doctorate in ecclesiology, as well as a deep ongoing interest in monastic and apophatic spirituality.

Janet Fletcher is Priest in the Bro Ystumanner Ministry Area in the Bangor Diocese, Church in Wales, and is also the Diocesan Spirituality Officer. She facilitates spiritual direction in the diocese and also offers spiritual direction herself. She has written *Pathway to God* (SPCK, 2006) and contributed to BRF's *Guidelines* Bible reading notes.

Andrea Skevington lives in Suffolk with her family. She writes for both adults and children, winning the Christian Book of the Year award (Speaking Volumes) for her retelling, *The Lion Classic Bible* (Lion Hudson, 2011). She also enjoys storytelling for children and running creative writing seminars for adults.

Sally Smith enjoys creating spaces that enable encounters with God through leading Quiet Days and creating prayer corners and stations. She has led prayer groups in her local church, works as a spiritual director, and writes and produces education materials.

Janet Lunt trained in music, composes, creates artwork and leads Quiet Days. She has designed several multisensory prayer trails, which have been used in Bristol, including in the cathedral, and beyond.

Dorinda Miller has been leading Quiet Days and retreats in the UK and overseas, across denominations, for many years. As well as running Staying in the Vine, a six-week course on prayer and spiritual disciplines, she is currently developing audio meditation resources for www.into-deeper-waters.com.

Lisa Cherrett is BRF's Project Editor and Managing Editor for Bible reading notes. She sings, writes haiku poetry and is interested in the relationship between Christianity and contemporary culture. She blogs at lisannie44.wordpress.com.

Liz Hoare is tutor in spiritual formation at Wycliffe Hall in Oxford. She teaches discipleship and prayer and has a special interest in spiritual direction. She is married to Toddy, a sculptor, and they have a son. Liz enjoys baking, the English countryside and looking after her chickens.

1–14 MAY

Sheep and shepherds

Fiona Stratta

YHWH (Jehovah) Rohi

Introduction

The word 'shepherd' is a translation of the Hebrew *rohi*. However, *rohi* embraces a wider meaning than this, for it is both a verb and a noun. As a noun it can mean 'pasture', 'friend', 'keeper' or 'companion' as well as 'shepherd', and as a verb it can mean 'to feed', 'to tend' or 'to lead to pasture'. The figurative language describing God as a shepherd reveals so much to us about the character of God. But when does this metaphor first appear in the Bible? We are familiar with the words of King David: 'The Lord is my Shepherd; I have all that I need' (Psalm 23:1, NLT). Yet more than 800 years before these words were penned, Jacob (a very successful sheep farmer and shepherd), when blessing his son Joseph, used the words 'the God who has been my shepherd all my life to this day' (Genesis 48:15). He refers to God as 'the Shepherd, the Rock of Israel' (49:24, NIV), the one who helps, blesses, feeds and sustains us physically, emotionally and spiritually. Jacob had discovered that he had the weakness and vulnerability of a wandering sheep and that he needed to have complete dependence on God, the Shepherd, for sustenance and provision. Moses also spent many years working as a shepherd; his relationship with the God who spoke to him as a *rohi*—friend (Exodus 33:11)—speaks of closeness. From the beginning of the Bible to its end, individual 'sheep' discover intimacy with their Shepherd, 'For the Lamb at the centre of the throne will be their shepherd' (Revelation 7:17).

Sheep and shepherds

> *Jehovah Rohi*
> *Our companion on life's journey,*
> *Our friend and guide,*
> *Our keeper and protector,*
> *Feed us from your abundant supply,*
> *Tend to our wounds, Good Shepherd,*
> *Lead us to green and spacious places,*
> *For we are your people, the sheep of your pasture.*
>
> Inspired by Psalm 100 and by the prayer 'Good Shepherd' from *The Edge of Glory: Prayers in the Celtic tradition* by David Adam (SPCK, 1985)

You may like to write your own prayer at the start of this series as a 'sheep' to the 'Shepherd', perhaps using Psalm 100 as a starting place.

The Shepherd leads

Going out

> *He lets me rest in green meadows;*
> *he leads me beside peaceful streams.*
> *He renews my strength.*
>
> PSALM 23:2–3, NLT

In the West we are accustomed to seeing shepherds with their dogs driving and herding the flocks from behind. However, the ancient Near Eastern shepherd *led* his flock. We need to remember that God does not drive us, but leads us. It is always our choice whether we follow him or whether we wander off on another path. The shepherd had his crook at hand which he used to encourage the sheep to stay with him.

Reflect on times in your life when you have known the shepherd's crook (or staff) gently holding you back from wandering off the path, guiding you along the 'right paths, bringing honour to his name' (Psalm 23:3, NLT).

We need to be led to places of rest and peace. Rest is one of our most basic requirements, but one that 21st-century living can so easily squeeze out. Our Shepherd knows that both rest and the beauty of the natural world restore us. Take yourself off to a place where you can enjoy the refreshment of walking in green fields, preferably where there are 'quiet waters', be it a stream, river, pond or lake. Let the serenity of this walk calm and renew you. If weather permits, sit in the shade of a tree and consider how the shepherd of ancient times searched for a shady spot where he and the sheep could rest in the heat of the day. There they were free to graze, drink water and enjoy the security of being near the shepherd. While delighting in their contentment, the shepherd kept an eye out for anything that would disturb their well-being. Meditate on these words:

The Lord himself watches over you!
The Lord stands beside you as your protective shade.
PSALM 121:5, NLT

Reflect on times when you have been aware of the Lord watching over you and providing 'shade' in the heat of life's experiences.

If you are unable to go for a walk, find a picture online or in a book that stills your mind and then carry out the above reflection. One possibility is the painting *Seated Shepherdess* by Jean-François Millet.

Sheep and shepherds

The Shepherd restores our souls

Creative

> *He restores my soul.*
> PSALM 23:3, NIV 1984

> *Once you were like sheep who wandered away. But now you have turned to your Shepherd, the Guardian of your souls.*
> 1 PETER 2:25, NLT

The Shepherd desires not only to bring us physical and mental rest, but also to bring wholeness to our soul; his work encompasses restoring, reviving, renewing, redeeming and releasing us. Take a piece of paper and two pens of different colours. Make headings: Restore, Revive, Renew, Redeem, Release. In one colour record ways in which God has restored, revived, renewed, redeemed and released you. In the other colour write down areas in which you would like to see your soul being made increasingly whole—parts of your life where you need restoration, revival, renewal or release, and situations or relationships that need to be redeemed. Bring these to God in prayer.

David was not only a shepherd but also a gifted musician. He was called to play his harp to King Saul when the king was distressed. As Saul found out, listening to restful music is one way of calming a troubled soul (1 Samuel 16:23). There are numerous beautiful renditions of Psalm 23 to suit every musical taste. Why not listen to one of these, letting the words restore your trust, peace and hope? Some examples are 'The King of Love my Shepherd is' by H.W. Baker; 'The Lord is my Shepherd' by Howard Goodall; 'The Lord is my Shepherd' by John Rutter; 'The Lord's my Shepherd, I'll not want' by Stuart Townend.

Alternatively, you could listen to some soothing pastoral classical music, such as J.S. Bach's *Sheep May Safely Graze*.

Many of the psalms end with a declaration of trust in God and with the writer finding stability and peace amid difficulties. Psalm 23 ends with the words, 'Surely your goodness and unfailing love will pursue me all the days of my life, and I will live in the house of the Lord forever' (NLT). Repeat these words to yourself (or sing them) at various points throughout the day, facilitating their journey from your head to your heart.

The Shepherd protects and provides

Reflective

> *Even when I walk through the darkest valley,*
> *I will not be afraid,*
> *for you are close beside me.*
> *Your rod and your staff*
> *protect and comfort me.*
>
> PSALM 23:4, NLT

Sheep are unaware of the dangers around them: precipices, rocks and thorns, poisonous plants and wild animals. However, the shepherd is attentive to them all. An essential part of the job of a Near Eastern shepherd involved protecting the flock by day and by night. The shepherd's rod (or club) was often the root end of a small tree, useful for driving off animals threatening the flock. The shepherd's staff (crook) had many uses: to draw a sheep close to the shepherd, perhaps for examination; to lift a separated lamb back to its mother; to bring back a sheep about to wander off; to guide the sheep through a gate; to rescue a fallen sheep or one entrapped in thorns. The shepherd would have been extremely strong as a result of the toughness of his daily life. He devoted his strength to the care and well-being of his sheep.

We read in Psalm 28:8 that 'The Lord is the strength of his people'. Sheep are powerless to protect themselves, and a lone sheep is particularly vulnerable. In an age where so many people value independence and self-sufficiency, it is wise to reflect on our utter dependence on the Lord, our Shepherd, and to recognise our reliance on both the created world and other people.

How many people have been (or will be) involved in your day? List not only the people you have had contact with, but also the unknown: those involved in the chain of bringing food to our tables and clothes to our shops; those involved in our travel and leisure. Your list is unique to your circumstances; use it as a springboard to prayers of gratitude for the many ways, both large and small, in which we are blessed each day and for these many signs of God's loving care.

The Near Eastern shepherd would guide his flock not only to green pastures but also through deep ravines and gullies where there was little daylight. Our 'darkest valley' (Psalm 23:4) could be bereavement ('the valley of the shadow of death'), but could also be pain or illness, mental anguish or heartache, fear or profound disappointment. The Shepherd, our companion, guides us through these valleys to what awaits us on the other side both in this life and beyond, where we will 'dwell in the house of the Lord for ever' (v. 6).

The Shepherd anoints

Meditative

> *You anoint my head with oil;*
> *my cup overflows.*
> PSALM 23:5

The Near Eastern shepherd carried a pouch of oil. If a sheep became caught in brambles or cut on rocks, the shepherd rubbed healing oil onto the injured area.

Oil was essential in biblical times for cooking, for medicinal purposes, for light and for trade. It is a symbol found throughout the Bible.

If you have a burner with essential oils, prepare this. Then, while you enjoy the fragrance, follow through this meditation on oil. Alternatively, you could rub some oil on your forehead.

- Oil is a symbol for healing in the Bible. Leaders are instructed to pray for the sick, anointing them with oil (James 5:14). Jesus is the great Physician who binds our wounds.

Good Shepherd, bring healing to our bodies, minds and souls.

- Anointing with oil is also a sign of being chosen (set apart) as a leader by God. Priests were anointed for God's purposes, as were kings. Jesus was God's 'anointed one' (see Psalm 2:2), fulfilling Isaiah's prophecy, 'The Spirit of the Sovereign Lord is on me, because the Lord has anointed me to preach good news to the poor. He has sent me to bind up the broken-hearted, to proclaim freedom for the captives and release from darkness for the prisoners' (Isaiah 61:1, NIV 1984).

Anointed One, anoint us so that we may fulfil your purposes for our lives.

- Oil is a symbol for gladness. 'God, your God, has anointed you, pouring out the oil of joy on you' (Psalm 45:7 and Hebrews 1:9, NLT). When the Lord brings comfort, he bestows 'the oil of gladness instead of mourning' (Isaiah 61:3, NIV 1984).

Our Shepherd, give us the joy of the Lord to strengthen us.

- Oil symbolises the presence of the Holy Spirit who energises us. Perhaps you can recall the chorus 'Give me oil in my lamp, keep me burning'. We need to go on being filled with the Spirit (Ephesians 5:18) in order to live according to God's ways and purposes as we await Christ's return. You may like to include the parable of the ten bridesmaids at the start of Matthew 25 as part of your meditation.

Anointed One, our Shepherd-King, fill us with your Spirit.

The Shepherd comforts

Going out

At the end of the day the Near Eastern shepherd could be seen carrying a tired lamb across his shoulders or in his arms, while the mother sheep walked closely beside him. The shepherd had a particular care for the most helpless: the young and their mothers.

We read in the book of Isaiah, 'He tends his flock like a shepherd: he gathers the lambs in his arms and carries them close to his heart; he gently leads those that have young' (40:11).

While in the Lake District I watched a shepherd attend to some ewes and their lambs that were just a few days old. Try to find an opportunity to walk by a field of ewes and their lambs. Watch their behaviour and consider how the shepherd gives special attention to these vulnerable members of the flock. Think of those who are defenceless in our society or who need special care in our communities and churches. Are there any ways we can participate in 'pastoral' care? Jesus gave us the 'new commandment' to love one another in the way that he has loved us (John 13:34). In this sense we are all to aspire to the development of a pastoral heart.

Perhaps you are feeling particularly vulnerable at the moment. If so, meditate on these verses:

> *The Lord is close to the broken-hearted*
> *and saves those who are crushed in spirit.*
> PSALM 34:18

> *A bruised reed he will not break,*
> *and a smouldering wick he will not snuff out.*
> ISAIAH 42:3

Do not be afraid to ask for pastoral support, remembering that our Shepherd's tender, loving care often comes to us through other people.

The Good Shepherd who lays down his life

Reflective

> *'I am the good shepherd. I know my own sheep, and they know me.'*
> JOHN 10:14, NLT

In the Bible the metaphor of the shepherd was also used for the leaders of the Israelites; some had been unfaithful shepherds who had failed to care for the flock. Jesus referred to himself as the Good Shepherd, therefore claiming to be a leader of the people, in fact *the* Leader of the people, the one who fulfilled the long-awaited prophecy, 'I will place over them one shepherd, my servant David, and he will tend them; he will tend them and be their shepherd' (Ezekiel 34:23). Jesus criticised those leaders who had led the sheep astray, who, rather than caring for them, had abandoned them. In the ancient Near East it was not unheard-of for hired shepherds to run away from danger when the crunch came, but the good shepherd, one who was true and faithful, would fight off any intruder, even to the extent of giving his life for the sheep.

Jesus said, 'I am the good shepherd. The good shepherd sacrifices his life for the sheep' (John 10:11, NLT). We know that Christ did this for us when he was crucified at Calvary, reconciling us to God.

There are many images online of the Good Shepherd with his sheep. In some he is carrying a sheep or lamb; in others he is being followed by his sheep. Some icons have a cross behind the shepherd, signifying what lay ahead for Jesus. In one particularly moving Greek icon of *Christ the Good Shepherd*, the Shepherd is carrying a person on his shoulders in place of a lamb. If you are able to, look at these and allow them to speak to you.

You may prefer to read the poem 'Footsteps in the Sand' by Mary Stevenson, which reminds us that when we are at our weakest, the Good Shepherd carries us (Psalm 28:9).

The door/gate

Meditative

> *'I am the gate; whoever enters through me will be saved. He will come in and go out, and find pasture.'*
> JOHN 10:9, NIV 1984

The Near Eastern sheepfold consisted of a square stone enclosure, often with thorns at the top of the wall to keep out wild animals and thieves. The shepherd would sleep in the gateway, becoming the door guarding the flock. Nothing could enter without passing over him. Several flocks may have shared one fold, so in the morning each shepherd would call his sheep by name. The sheep, recognising their shepherd's voice from their daily contact with him, would come at his call and follow him out of the fold to find pasture.

We read of this daily watchfulness in Psalm 121:8 (ESV): 'The Lord will keep your going out and your coming in from this time forth and forevermore.' Such knowledge enables us to live with a deep peace, knowing that we can rely on God's care. Jesus promised such peace to his followers.

Meditate on these words of prophecy:

He will stand and shepherd his flock in the strength of the Lord,
in the majesty of the name of the Lord his God.
And they will live securely, for then his greatness
will reach to the ends of the earth.
And he will be their peace.

MICAH 5:4–5, NIV 1984

The Shepherd rescues

Reflective

On a cycle ride in Snowdonia, we came across a distressed sheep that had somehow left the field and could find no way back to the flock. My husband eventually managed to pick it up, no mean feat, and return it to the field. This picture of 'rescue' has stayed with me.

As darkness fell, the Near Eastern shepherd led his flock to the fold. He then stood at the door counting them as they came through, passing under his rod. If one was missing, he would set out to find it. In one of the most familiar stories that Jesus told (Luke 15:3–7), the shepherd left 99 sheep in order to look for the missing one. When he found the sheep, he placed it on his shoulders and joyfully carried it back. In this story we are reminded that although the shepherd considers the flock's requirements as a whole, he is also concerned with the needs of each individual lamb or sheep.

The parable ends, not with the return of the sheep to the fold, but with the shepherd celebrating its safe return with his friends. We read in Psalm 18:19 (NLT) that our Shepherd delights in our well-being: 'He led me to a place of safety; he rescued me because he delights in me.'

Think of a time when you have found something precious or important that you thought lost. The relief and joy increases beyond measure if it is a loved one who has returned home safely. Awareness of our weakness can keep us from realising the great delight that our Shepherd takes in us. What in your life is the Lord delighting in? What has he rescued you from? What dangers and fears does the 'fold' protect you from?

Pray that you may be enfolded in the Shepherd's love and kept in his fold.

All we like sheep

Creative

The Lord is the Shepherd and we are the sheep—if nothing else this should humble us! I asked a shepherd, Phil Childs, what he considered to be the characteristics of sheep. He responded: 'scatty', 'timid', 'lacking in trust' and 'apprehensive'. Phil explained that sheep in Western flocks tend not to create a relationship with the shepherd because of the size of the flock. However, he recounted the story of Teasel, a Southdown sheep reared by hand. She was unafraid of human contact, came when called and would follow him anywhere. Teasel loved to be petted and shown affection. Such was her confidence as a result of this attention that she could star without a tether in nativity plays!

Re-read the traits of sheep listed above. Write down ways and times when you have reacted like a sheep that doesn't 'know' its shepherd. Now read Psalm 100:3: 'Know that the Lord is God. It is he who made us, and we are his; we are his people, the sheep of his pasture.'

We are known and loved by God as individuals, given his care and attention that has the potential to release in us the qualities seen in Teasel: the ability to love and be loved; a trust in the Shepherd that drives away our natural fear; a desire to follow him wherever he leads and the confidence to participate in life in ways we would not have thought possible! Now write down ways in which you have seen God's love enabling you to flourish. Jesus, our Good Shepherd, tells us that he came so that we 'may have life, and have it to the full' (John 10:10).

We tend to miss out when we fail to respond to the Shepherd by not following his lead and example. Isaiah wrote, 'We all, like sheep, have gone astray, each of us has turned to our own way; and the Lord has laid on him the iniquity of us all' (Isaiah 53:6). Listen to these words being sung in Handel's *Messiah*, which brings them to life so powerfully.

The Lamb of God

Music

We cannot consider sheep and shepherds without dwelling on the truth that Jesus was not only the Good Shepherd but also the Lamb of God. John the Baptist, when he saw Jesus approaching, said 'Look! The Lamb of God who takes away the sin of the world!' (John 1:29, NLT).

Sheep and lambs were important commodities in biblical times. They provided food and wool, and their hides were used to make leather goods. Lambs were also needed for sacrifice. Each morning and evening a perfect lamb was sacrificed at the temple for the sins of the people—in order to pay the penalty for sin a life had to be given. Isaiah prophesied, 'He was led like a lamb to the slaughter' (Isaiah 53:7, NLT). Jesus became the final sacrifice, giving his life to take away the sins of the world (John 3:16).

In faith we look ahead to the time when Christ will finally be

Sheep and shepherds

both lamb and shepherd. 'For the lamb on the throne will be their Shepherd. He will lead them to springs of life-giving water. And God will wipe every tear from their eyes' (Revelation 7:17, NLT).

Listen to the two contrasting pieces from Handel's *Messiah*: the words of promise combined with a sense of the suffering to come in 'Behold the Lamb of God', and the words of triumph in 'Worthy is the Lamb that was slain'.

Psalm 23

Poetry

At my Christian writers' group, we were given the challenge of rewriting the 23rd psalm, using a different metaphor. I chose to use the metaphor 'sherpa', feeling slightly concerned that I was using such a humble, although essential, role with which to compare the King of kings and Lord of lords. It almost felt irreverent. I then realised that, in calling Yahweh his Shepherd, David had done exactly this, for shepherding (although of vital importance) was humble work. Jesus, the Good Shepherd, explained to his disciples that he came not to be served, but to serve and to give his life. He described himself as gentle and humble, the one who gives rest to our souls.

> *The Lord is my Sherpa,*
> *He has all I need.*
> *He ensures I take breaks at regular intervals*
> *And leads me through breathtaking scenery.*
> *He guides me in his wisdom and knowledge*
> *Along the best paths that only a sherpa knows.*
> *Even though I walk through narrow gorges and*
> *Climb the steepest mountain paths,*
> *I will not be afraid,*

Sheep and shepherds

> *For you are close beside me,*
> *Carrying my load, training me, encouraging me.*
> *You set up camp and feed me in the middle of hostile environments,*
> *I have more than enough to eat and drink, the healthiest food and purest water.*
> *You gently massage my sore muscles and aching head,*
> *You soothe my blistered feet.*
> *I know that your unstinting kindness and compassion will always be with me,*
> *Supporting me from behind until I end this journey.*
> *Then I will travel no more, but live with you, rest with you*
> *For ever.*

Why not finish this series by writing your own version of Psalm 23?

> *Shepherd of our souls, we thank you that your goodness and mercy will follow us as we follow you.*
> *Amen*

15–28 MAY

St Benedict

John Fitzmaurice

Listening

Introduction

The Rule of St Benedict is one of the classic texts of Western Christendom and indeed of Western civilisation. Written in the sixth century, it wasn't the first monastic rule to be written; indeed scholars believe it to be significantly derived from an anonymous rule entitled 'The Rule of the Master', but it was the first to gain widespread influence, an influence it has retained throughout the centuries. Benedict himself is considered to be the father of Western monasticism, not least due to the influence of the Rule. Parts of the Rule can feel quite alien to the modern reader, but as a whole it remains an inspirational document full of wisdom and realism for those trying to live the Christian life in a variety of contexts.

The first word of the opening Prologue sets the tone. 'Listen…' says Benedict. This attitude of listening is identified by Benedict, and by many of the other great writers and teachers in the spiritual tradition, as being what undergirds a God-focused life. If we are to know God, if we are to respond to God, then we must first listen. So today you are invited to listen, to listen deeply. You can do this anywhere—it doesn't need to be in a quiet space, though that might help. Simply listen to everything you can hear going on around and within you. Just notice the noises; don't evaluate them. What are the prominent sounds, and what are the ones that belong more in the background? Listen to your body. How do you feel? Are you tense or anxious? Listen to the sound of your breath as it enters and exits your body. Listen also to your thoughts as they rush around in your head—don't process them, just listen. Slowly and over a period of some time, listen deeply, and become present to all that is going on around you and within you, and you will become fully present to the present moment, and that's where we meet God.

Stability

Going out

We live in a fragmented world and indeed in a fragmented church. This fragmentation is sometimes caused by an abundance of choice—we never really settle because we think someone else might be having more fun than we are, that the grass on the other side of the hill might be greener. This can be paralysing, as it makes us restless and disturbed people. We never fully commit to things or to people, because we think a better option might come along and we will be trapped.

It was the same in Benedict's time, not least among those who claimed to live the monastic life, and in Chapter 1 of the Rule Benedict is disparaging of certain kinds of monks who live in ways of which he disapproves. Benedict insists that his monks make a vow of stability, that they commit to the community for the rest of their lives, and that generally means committing to a particular monastery in a particular place… for the rest of their lives. There is no option to go and live in another monastery because a monk is bored with his current one. The commitment is for good.

This is deeply countercultural in our fluid, consumer society, so today try putting down roots where you are, even if it's only for a short time. Walk slowly around your flat, or your house; walk around your garden or the perimeter of your property; or maybe prayer walk some of your local streets. Feel what it means to be present at this time in this place. Imagine the people who have made this place what it is today. Who do you share this place with now? What do you bring—how will this place be better for the fact that you have been here? In Jesus, God became present in a particular place at a particular time. What's God up to where you are, and how can you join in?

Conversion of life

Creative

The next vow Benedict asks his monks to make is that of *conversatio morum*, which is difficult to translate, but is broadly 'conversion of life'. This is the flip side of stability because it reminds us that when we embrace stability and put down roots, then we can grow; indeed there is no virtue in stability for its own sake, only in that it allows us to grow.

I wonder if you can identify growth in your life. How have you changed in the past five or ten years? What has changed and what has stayed the same? In a healthy life there will be both consistency and development. Do you feel stuck in a rut? Or perhaps there's been so much change you feel it all needs to be rooted in some more stable time. Either way, Benedict reminds us that by balancing stability with conversion of life, we can feel safe enough to grow and change and develop as we slowly become closer to the people God created us to be.

One way of tracing your growth and development is to look through old collections of photographs, or scrapbooks. If you have regularly kept a journal or reflective diary, you might want to re-read what you have written in those. Alternatively, you might like to write out or draw your life story. You can do this sequentially by listing significant dates, events and people; or you can be creative and paint or draw representations of key moments in your life, trying to capture their emotional impact and even seeking connections between them. Look back on the journey you have been on, which God has walked with you, and ask for his guidance in what he might be calling you to next. How are you being called to develop in the next five or ten years? What will remain consistent, and what needs to change?

Obedience

Reflective/creative

The third vow to which Benedict calls his monks is that of obedience. Obedience is important in the spiritual life because it is through obedience that we create the environment in which we can grow. Obedience is ultimately about being liberated from our emotions, our feelings and even our whims. This doesn't mean that our emotions, feelings or urge to spontaneity are bad things—far from it; they are vital parts of our lives which we must stay aware of and in dialogue with. Obedience simply reminds us that we must not be controlled by them. Obedience means doing certain things even if we don't particularly want to at that time, and we do so because we realise that ultimately those things are the right thing to do in the long run. Thus obedience and discipline are closely connected.

Obedience and discipline often carry negative and joyless connotations, but the reality is different. Obedience and discipline, while initially being demanding and even inconvenient, ultimately are liberating and freeing as we discover we are not victim to our instincts and that we can choose the better way.

I wonder if there is something nagging in the back of your head that you know you really should do, but that you keep putting off. It might be finding more time for prayer, or spending more time studying scripture; it might be visiting a neighbour or helping in the community in some way; it might be to do with your own physical, mental or emotional well-being. Identify something that you have been putting off, and commit to doing it. If it feels too huge, then break it down into a series of little actions and tick them off one by one. I promise you will feel a great sense of achievement when you complete your task, not just because the task is completed, but because you have overcome the voices in you that have prevented you from doing it in the first place. Obedience and discipline are all about self-mastery, and self-mastery is not an end in itself but rather a tool that allows us to offer ourselves more fully and more totally to God.

Lectio divina

Meditative

Lectio divina is one of the most characteristic aspects of Benedictine spirituality. The practice of *lectio* did not originate with Benedict, but in Chapter 48 of his Rule he prescribes its use at particular times throughout the day, and its practice has flourished within Benedictine spirituality and in recent years has been made accessible to a wider non-monastic audience. Benedict's approach to *lectio divina* or 'divine (or spiritual) reading' connects us back to his first injunction to listen. This is a way of engaging with the scriptures which isn't about logical or rational learning or indeed didactic teaching; this is a way of listening to scripture (and by extension to many other things) that engages the heart. In the practice of *lectio* we listen with our heart to what God is saying to us through the words of scripture.

There are slightly different ways of describing the process of *lectio*. Generally, it consists of four activities that take place in sequence, though the experience of many is that the process isn't always neatly linear. Simply put, it works like this:

1. Choose a passage of scripture to read, and read it through very slowly and thoughtfully. Feel the shape of the words and phrases; hear their resonance.
2. From this passage pick a word or a phrase that jumps out for you, one that seems particularly meaningful or appropriate or just curious. Once you've done this you can discard the rest of the passage. Slowly examine the word or phrase that the Holy Spirit has given you; repeat it over and over again. Why did these words strike you? What is God telling you through them? What insight do these words hold for you at this particular time? This activity has been compared to sucking a boiled sweet—slowly extracting the flavour from the text.
3. Having discerned what you think God is giving you through these words, consider what your response to that gift might be. It might simply be an inner response of deeper understanding, or you might want to do something now or later.
4. The final aspect of *lectio* is simply to rest for a short time in gratitude that God speaks to us through the scriptures.

Hospitality

Reflective

Another key component of Benedictine spirituality is that of hospitality. In Chapter 53 of his Rule, Benedict urges that guests who arrive at the monastery should be received as if they were Christ himself. Here Benedict lives out Jesus' injunction in Matthew 25:35b: 'I was a stranger and you welcomed me' (NRSV). This attitude of hospitality opens us up to the possibility of meeting Christ in everyone we meet without distinction; the beggar will be welcomed with the same honour and care as the ecclesiastical dignitary. Here, too, are echoes of Benedict's opening injunction to listen—listen to all states of people and we will find Christ hidden in them. A spirituality of hospitality invites us to use the same process with people that we use with scripture in *lectio*—what is God offering me in this particular person at this particular time and how might I respond?

When we begin to see others as angels or messengers of God who come to both comfort and disturb us, who call us to new understandings and new tasks, then we approach people in new and different ways. We realise that those whom we find difficult might be important for us on our journey; they might call out from us a level of forgiveness, of tolerance or compassion that we have hereto been unwilling to give. We may be being called to see a situation from the point of view of another, and to step out of our comfort zone to get new insight, new understanding.

Who do you need to be hospitable to? Who do you need to welcome as Christ? Perhaps there is someone you should invite to your house or someone you should visit in their home. Perhaps there is someone you just need to spend time with, stepping beyond your feelings for them and listening deeply to them, seeing in them the image of Christ. Think who that person might be and arrange to spend time with them in the next day or two.

Work

Reflective

For those who have had little contact with the monastic life there is always the temptation to see it as 'very spiritual', an endless round of chanting and mystical experiences. While, depending on the community, there may be a bit of both, monastic life is, in reality, deeply earthed.

Benedict was emphatic that all members of the community who are able must contribute to the manual work of the monastery. He writes, 'Idleness is the enemy of the soul…' Yet Benedict is not a hard taskmaster—the work assigned to each member must be appropriate for his or her 'constitution'. This placing of manual work at the heart of the life of a community committed to the gospel might seem puzzling to some, but here again we see Benedict's wisdom and his understanding of the spiritual life. Unlike the attitude of some in contemporary society, who see work as a necessary evil, Benedict realises that appropriate, meaningful work nourishes the soul—it gives to human life purpose, achievement and dignity as well as being an outlet for the innate creativity that is intrinsic to human life. The manual work of the monastery, our day-to-day chores at home, and whatever professional work we may or may not do are means of grace, ways in which we can partake in the creativity of God. It is worth saying that modes of work in society that demean human dignity and creativity need to be challenged and rejected.

So today you don't need to do anything you wouldn't normally be doing; you just need to do it with a different understanding. How can the tasks you aim to achieve today, be they professional or domestic, be means of grace, places of encounter with the creativity of God where you can grow in your humanity and your soul is expanded?

Opus Dei—the Daily Office

Creative/liturgy

Benedict's monks met together, and those who today live the Benedictine life in community continue to meet together seven times a day to pray corporately. The daily round of offices, starting with the night office of Vigils and ending with Compline, punctuates the day at regular intervals with prayer. Whatever tasks are being undertaken are put on pause or stopped to honour the primary calling of the monastic and indeed Christian life, that of worship.

The effect of the Daily Office is to sanctify time—it's about listening to the rhythms of the day and of our bodies and contextualising them in prayer and worship.

The night office of Vigils is a time of waiting, of listening and expectation. Lauds (Morning Prayer) is a time of praise and delight for the new day, the fulfilment of God's promises as the darkness passes, giving way to light and new possibilities. Terce marks the beginning of the workday, offering all that we do to God, while Sext is said at midday in the midst of all our busyness, again contextualising all that we do within prayer and worship. The afternoon begins with None as we begin to wind down and head towards the evening. Vespers (Evening Prayer) marks the end of the workday and the entry into the rest and relaxation of evening, and finally Compline (Night Prayer) marks the completion of the day as night takes hold and the cycle begins once again. (For a longer explanation of this, see C.V. Paintner, *The Artist's Rule: Nurturing your creative soul with monastic wisdom,* Sorin Books, 2011.)

This oscillation between prayer and work synchronises the rhythms of our bodies and of the day; it sanctifies our work, our rest and our lives. What are the rhythms in your life, in your day, in your week? Note the times of busyness and of relaxation, of beginnings and of endings, and find a way to contextualise them in prayer. You could try a simple Daily Office, or simply offer a short prayer or time of reflection at particular times of the day.

Silence

Prayer

Benedictine spirituality is characterised by balance and by moderation—a balance between work and prayer, between community and solitude. Within the daily round of work and prayer there is the potential for much busyness. Benedict recognises the need for times of rest, both physical and spiritual. This spiritual rest is achieved in silence. In Chapter 42 of the Rule, Benedict says that silence should be sought at all times by monks and nuns, and this is especially important at night-time. Among all the busyness and words of the day, now is a time for silence. This brings us back to Benedict's starting point of listening. We listen to the world around us, we listen to the life within us, to the gift of God in scripture and in other people, to the insights gained through our work; but now is a time for a different type of listening. Silence invites us to a deeper listening, to the depths of God that exist beneath our surface activity. In silence we are invited to sink deeply into the inexpressible mystery of God that transcends words and activity. Here we are held and renewed.

Silence means passing through our awareness of our surroundings into something deeper. We sit quietly and comfortably to allow our bodies to be silent; we reduce external stimuli as much as possible… and then many of us find that our brains go into overdrive! 'Now that I've got your attention…' our brains seem to say before filling our minds with hundreds of thoughts and concerns. We need to silence these as well, but this can be tricky. To silence our minds, we need to let go of our thoughts… just let them drift away. If you have an important thought that you don't want to lose, quickly write it down so it's safe, and then let it drift away. There is a pain barrier for all who venture into silence, where the inner chatter seems to crescendo and then just fall away. The repetition of a short phrase or mantra can help focus the mind away from the chattering thoughts.

Find a time and place that allows you to be silent. Repeat the listening exercise in the introduction, but pass on into a deeper listening; listen to the silence of God.

Solitude

Reflective

Solitude goes hand in hand with silence. The experience of silence is a recognition of our solitude. Solitude is a casting away of all the false props of our lives, and concentration of ourselves into our very essence. But for many, solitude can feel threatening and scary. We live in a world where many are lonely and isolated, so why would we want to make a virtue out of solitude? It's important to distinguish between loneliness and solitude. Loneliness is a deep and painful ache inside a person that has its origins in feelings of not being accepted, not being understood, of being somehow incomplete; it is deeply destructive and is experienced by most people at different times in their lives, even when they have plenty of people around them. Solitude, however, is an affirming and nurturing place to be. The psychologist Donald Winnicott claimed that human maturity is evidenced by the ability to be alone in the presence of others. In solitude we feel complete. We are not dependent on others to make our lives meaningful; it's just us and God and that is enough. True solitude will help us realise the richness of our relationships and not their paucity.

Benedict's Rule is primarily written for monastics living in community, but he recognises that there are those who are called to live in greater solitude who have been prepared for the demands of such a life by their formation in community. Extended periods of solitude are not for everyone. However, if you live a busy frenetic life, try going off-grid for a couple of hours or even a day. Unplug or turn off the phone, disconnect from the internet and arrange to spend the day on your own, with none of your usual distractions. Allow yourself to go deep into the silence of such an experience, and if you are a person who is wrestling with loneliness, you might find that one of the gifts of solitude is the realisation that we are connected far more at a deep and profound level than we ever imagined.

Community

Intercession

Benedict expects that anyone drawn to solitude should first be formed in community. Paradoxically it was never Benedict's intention to form a religious community; he simply wanted to live the gospel as he understood it, and others were so inspired by his witness that they came to join him. However, it didn't always go well—one group of monks tried to poison him as they felt he was too demanding!

Community is difficult—any kind of community, be it family or church or workplace or neighbourhood. We have much in common as human beings, but we also have much that marks us out from each other. The gospel call is to a community of peace and reconciliation, one that reflects the mutual indwelling of the Holy Trinity. Learning to recognise Christ in visitor or guest is relatively easy compared to recognising him in the person you bump into first thing in the morning, or who has strong but differing opinions to you on issues that you are passionate about. Community forms and shapes us to be more compassionate, more considerate, more tolerant; it knocks some of the rough edges off us, and as we learn to be more accepting and less judgemental of others, so we actually learn to be more accepting and less judgemental of ourselves.

What communities do you belong to? Family, friends, neighbourhood, church, clubs and so on. Call them to mind and pray for them; give thanks that they tolerate and accept you, and pray that you may be more accepting and tolerant of them.

St Benedict

Rule 26

Reflective

This exploration of Benedictine spirituality has drawn on his Rule, a document that has shaped not only the communities that choose to live by it, but also the wider Western Church and Western society. However, for Benedict, and indeed for all the great monastic founders, the Rule was never an end in itself, but simply a guide to better living the gospel. The Rule should never become an excuse for legalism like that exhibited by the Pharisees, but should always serve to point beyond itself as a framework to liberate the believer to better live out their faith.

What framework would help you live out your faith? Would a few simple commitments help you keep focused on your faith on a day-to-day basis? A personal Rule of Life does not need to be as complicated as Benedict's, but rather can contain a few simple commitments about regular prayer (private and corporate), study (scripture and the Christian tradition more generally) and the service of others (in ways that are appropriate to your context).

Pray that God will guide you to create a framework for your life based on the practice of your faith. Don't be overambitious—just make a few simple commitments for a period of a month or two—and if it goes well you can always update and renew it. Perhaps you might share it with a trusted Christian friend or church minister who can hold you accountable to it.

29 MAY–11 JUNE

The prodigal

Janet Fletcher

The story

Introduction

Over the next two weeks we will explore, prayerfully, the story of the prodigal son; a story that is only found in the Gospel of Luke (15:11–32). This is a parable—a story with a deeper meaning and truth—and like an onion has many layers to unravel. We shall begin to unravel it a little over the coming days.

This parable inspired Rembrandt to paint *The Return of the Prodigal*; a painting, too, with many layers to explore, calling us to look beyond the surface to its inner meaning. The painting, like the parable, has a number of characters portrayed within its 'story'. The three main people are the younger son who wants to leave home, the older son who feels ignored, and the father who tries to do his best for each son.

The dictionary definition of 'prodigal' is someone who is wasteful, extravagant and a spendthrift, all of which describe the younger son. Each character in the parable offers a deeper exploration so that we can look and discern how each relates to us in our own lives, and how we may relate to them.

If you have a copy of, or are familiar with, the painting by Rembrandt (or try searching online), what strikes you most as you look at it? Is it the young son kneeling before his father? Is it the people hiding in the shadows? Or is it the figure of the father with both masculine and feminine hands?

Rembrandt depicts the father differently from the way in which

The prodigal

we may form an image of the person we read of in the Gospel. Yet the father figure is representing the person of God, and in a way that draws from both male and female imagery, and so will be referred to as the father/parent. What difference, if any, does this make for you when reading the parable in the Bible?

Take time to read through Luke 15:11–32.

What are your initial thoughts and feelings about the story?

Three perspectives

Reflective

Who are you? Are you a younger or older child, a middle child or an only child? Are you a parent? Whoever we are and whatever is the make-up of our family life and belonging, there will be different perspectives, different lenses through which life is lived, judged and viewed.

The parable of the prodigal son may be one that is many centuries away from our own, and from our understanding of society and the world today, yet within the story we see clearly the psychology of family dynamics at play. There is the younger son who wants his own way and the elder son who is somewhat miffed, petulant and annoyed at his younger brother and his father.

What is it like to be the eldest or the youngest in a family?

What is it like to be the parent who tries to keep all things equal between all children?

Each of the three main people in the story will have their own particular views and opinions. Each will see the unfolding events around them from the perspective of how it affects their own particular life and story; how it may change their life and story. In all families each member has a part to play. In all families there will be times of saying goodbye and times of welcoming back home.

Ponder your own family at different stages through your life—

when you were young and now at the present moment—and your part within it.

What, and when, have been your own experiences of times of 'goodbye'?

What, and when, have been your experiences of welcoming and being welcomed home?

The father/parent

Meditative

I look back to the day he left. He is my youngest son. Could he manage out there in a world full of temptation? With reluctance I gave in, and gave him his share of the inheritance which would be his when I am no longer here.

I didn't want him to go, but I knew I couldn't keep him with me. I knew that staying would cause a distance between us; he would become angry and frustrated, and would not care about the working of our land. I want the best for both my sons. I had to let him go. I cannot protect him, or my eldest, for ever. They need to find their own way in life, even if that breaks my heart.

I had no idea where he went, or what he did, until he poured it all out on his return home. This was a day I kept hoping for, but was never totally convinced would come. I waited and watched, still his father/parent.

Then that day came. I could hardly believe my eyes. I ran and ran towards him—most undignified for someone of my age and position! I ran. I didn't care. I held him, wrapped my arms around him. I dressed him in clean robes and put rings on his fingers, and gave him a party.

I didn't realise what my eldest would think. My youngest, who I felt had been dead, had now come home. He had found his way himself, and discovered what was important and true for living a good life.

The prodigal

- What life experiences have helped you to discover and learn more of who you are?
- How like the father/parent figure are you?
- Have you shared in any similar experiences?
- What does the father/parent figure reveal to you about God?
- Bring into a time of prayer children and adults who seem to be 'lost' from their families.

The tears

Poetry

The tears in the poem below are the tears of the younger son on arrival at his home, at the home where he hopes he will find a welcome. They could also be the tears shed by the father/parent watching out for the son's return. Tears often express the inner feelings for which we have few, if any, words.

> *Tears flow—downwards to the wet cheeks, unrestrained.*
> *Relief at the return home?*
> *Relief at being accepted back?*
> *Unexpected but so needed, these tears.*
> *There was no certainty of the welcome,*
> *and now?*
> *Emotions swirl around, rising to the surface*
> *from unexplored and hidden depths within*
> *to be expressed, only*
> *in a body yearning the touch, embrace, of a hug*
> *as tears flow.*
>
> *Tears which bypass the necessity of words,*
> *speak louder than any word,*
> *speaking, unspoken, of a love too deep*

*to put into words, only tears,
warm, genuine.*

*The restless heart has wandered far,
extravagantly, wasting opportunities given.
And now?
Hope, in the One who calls and guides,
waits with open arms, and cries
tears of eternal compassion,
unconditional love.*

Tears are not always a comfortable expression for some, as they lead us to become vulnerable. Yet tears can reveal inner strength and enable a deeper perspective and way forward to be discerned.

Are you comfortable with tears?

Are tears a part of your prayer life and relationship with God?

The elder son

Reflective

The image of the elder son is the opposite of the younger, prodigal son. The elder is hardworking; he obeys his father/parent by living a model life. With the return of the younger brother, the elder displays jealousy, becomes petulant, at the attention the other receives.

Was the elder son included in the conversations about his brother leaving and having his share of the inheritance at that time? What thoughts and feelings may the elder have had as he watched the younger pack and leave?

The elder son gives the impression of being full of duty and loyalty to his family and family home. Maybe this is why he never left to explore the wider world. Perhaps he was afraid to venture beyond the known and familiar. It may be that the younger did what the elder had often dreamt about, but lacked the courage to go out and do. Regardless of his hopes and dreams, the elder stays at home and works as he always has done and will do.

Unlike the father/parent, the elder son has not been willing to let his brother go and to encourage him to discover new things and experience life in different ways. Did the elder son ever believe the younger would return home again?

- How like the elder son are you?
- What does duty and loyalty mean to you? Is there room for self-growth and expression within these?
- Is there anything at the moment that you find difficult to let go of? This may be related to the home or workplace, or within the community of the church.
- Many find that they need to put others first in their daily lives—maybe as a carer. How do you ensure that this care is given out of love and not out of duty, in its most negative sense?

Packing?

Creative

The parable as Jesus tells it keeps some interesting pieces of information hidden. Did the younger son have a route planned out? Did he simply wander down the road to see where it would take him? What did he pack in his bag? Did he take a change of clothes, food to eat and something that reminded him of home? We can only speculate! The only definite item we know he took with him was his share of his inheritance, which he then squandered.

In a time of quietness and prayer, gather several small pieces of paper, or a very large sheet of paper, plus some coloured pencils. What would you pack for a journey? Using a separate piece of paper for each 'packing', or writing them all on one piece with different-coloured pencils, read through the list below, and write or draw what you would take with you.

- A day out. What would you pack for a day out—to a city or the country or the seaside?
- Going away. What would you pack for a long weekend away—in this country or abroad?
- A holiday. What would you pack for a one- or two-week holiday—in this country or abroad? (Some of the packing for a few days or a few weeks will probably be the same.)
- An emergency. If you had only 15 minutes, what are the most precious items you would pack? These might not be costly items in monetary terms but priceless through the memories they hold.
- In faith. What would you pack that would reveal to others your faith and journey with God?

Spend some time reflecting on all you have 'packed' into your different 'suitcases'.

End this time of quiet reflection by giving thanks to God for being a part of your journey through life.

The younger son

Reflective

The younger son is a risk-taker, seeking adventure. His father/parent could have denied him his share of the inheritance, but instead he has been set free. He can leave behind his life lived out within the boundaries of his family and the family property.

Had he thought about how his leaving would affect his father/parent or his elder brother, or about who would do his share of the

The prodigal

workload? Was he being selfish? No longer constrained, the world is his oyster! His adventure in life begins as he walks away from his home.

Eventually his adventure turns sour; he has wasted his money and is forced to take a job which takes away his freedom and independence. This is a turning point for the younger son. There is the realisation that at home the hired hands are looked after better than he is at that moment. It is also a moment of personal awareness and knowing the deep need to repent of all he has done to his father/parent. He will make amends. He will be a hired hand and not a son. He goes home.

What emotions and feelings would have been rolling around inside him on that journey home? Was there a sense of confusion and bewilderment as he saw his father/parent run to him? How did he feel as he tried to repent amid the preparations of a party in his honour?

Our own journey through life may not have been as adventurous or as extravagant as that of the younger son, but we will all have had times of leaving and times of coming home. Sometimes these are planned and arranged, and at other times they happen unexpectedly. Some of these may be difficult and painful, others joyful and eagerly looked forward to.

- What are your experiences of 'leaving' and 'returning'?
- Which of these are a part of your home life, family life, work life, church life and your relationship with God?
- How did it feel to 'leave' and how did it feel to 'return'?
- What changed within you as a result of 'leaving' and 'returning'?

The hug

Poetry

When the younger son arrived home, he was welcomed with a hug. What is a hug and what does it mean to you? A hug can reveal…

- an acknowledgement of another person in welcome
- the sharing of love and affection
- an empathetic awareness of another's needs

It offers a moment of close contact and can bring a sense of hope, healing and reassurance.

This is the initial contact between the father/parent and the prodigal. You may wish to pray it by placing yourself as either the father/parent or the prodigal.

> *Unrestrained, ready*
> *are the arms*
> *stretched out to the limit*
> *drawing me closer, and closer still,*
> *until embraced in a hug of love.*
> *The intimate unconditional love*
> *which brings forth life.*
> *Hugged so close that the tears well up,*
> *pour out, soak*
> *the other's shoulder, hair.*
> *A hug where bodies meet, two as one*
> *in comfort giving, arms entwined*
> *in welcome forgiveness,*
> *no questions asked, tears tell the story.*
> *A hug, personal, private, yet*
> *public to all on the open road.*

> *Who drew whom into this hug?*
> *A hug in which there is great longing*
> *to be drawn into the arms of the one and One*
> *who is both physical strength and*
> *profound tenderness.*
> *Warmed, welcomed in this hug,*
> *life can be lived, and loved once more.*

- Read through this poem prayerfully. Is there anything you feel uncomfortable with? Why?
- Is there a word or a phrase that seems important to you?
- Imagine that you are the one giving God a hug. What does that feel like?
- Imagine that you are being hugged by God. What does that feel like?
- Reflect upon the times when you have been given, or have given, a hug from a family member or friend, or prayerfully from God. What were those times and how did a hug help you and the other person?

The reality of life

Reflective

The younger son met the reality of life head on, and found that it was not quite as he imagined it to be. Or perhaps that the journey through life and the choices made are, or can be, determined by those we associate with.

Facing the reality of life can be difficult and painful, whether this is from the perspective of what is local to us, or seen from across the world. Looking at life around us can lead us to a place of despair, and 'empathy overload' from all we see and hear in the news. It may lead to a 'switching off' and disengagement through a sense of helplessness to do anything to help.

The younger son soon found that once his wealth had gone no one was interested in him. He became a displaced person. Penniless and homeless, he took a menial job. This is a reality for many today—taking a job for which they are overqualified, simply to have money to pay their own way. We see this displacement in different ways, from refugees and migrants seeking a place of safety, to young people trying to find work after gaining a university degree, and many others too.

Displacement, particularly perhaps for those who have fled areas of the world where they faced death or imprisonment, can also mean they are offered little or no welcome, little or no shelter, little or no money or support. What can we do?

The younger son was fortunate, as he had a home to go back to. Yet unexpected was the welcome home he received. The reality of life here is one where love overcomes all obstacles, all questions, all answers, and simply accepts and welcomes.

- How welcoming are you, and your church, to those who may be described as displaced?
- How welcoming are you, and your church, to those whose ideals, opinions, way of living are different from your own?
- How may the reality of life—its welcome and its harshness—be brought more deeply into your personal prayer and into the prayer and mission of your church?

The welcome

Liturgy

In a time of quietness, read through the prayer below quickly and then slowly return to each part, and before making the response, offer your own personal thoughts to God in prayer, seeking help,

The prodigal

asking for guidance, calling upon the gifts of the Holy Spirit.

God says: I call out to you in love, and I welcome you into my heart and life. I welcome your faith.

Pray for a deepening of faith and of calling, and an understanding of God in your life.

I welcome you, O God. Make me worthy of your love and call in my life.

God says: I have watched over you as you have sought out your path in life. I welcome your courage.

Pray for the courage to live and be the person you are known to be by God.

I welcome you, O God. Make me worthy of your oversight and care in my life.

God says: I have heard the words you have spoken from the depths of your inner being. I welcome your repentance.

Pray for the seeking of forgiveness and for wisdom in speaking.

I welcome you, O God. Make me worthy of your forgiving love in my life.

God says: I see within you the seeds of potential bursting to come into fruitfulness. I welcome your growing service.

Pray for nurturing of the giftedness blessed to you from God.

I welcome you, O God. Make me worthy of your nurturing presence in my life.

Writing your own prayer

Creative

Begin by reading through the parable of the prodigal son in Luke 15:11–32.

Take time to become still in the presence of God and allow the words of the parable to float around you, taking them deeper within, seeking from them words and images for prayer.

What would your prayer to God be, from the perspective of the father/parent, of the elder son and of the younger son?

What would your prayer to God be, taken from your own thoughts and feelings after reading this parable?

The prayer or prayers can be long or short, and can be…

- formed by random words or phrases
- structured or unstructured
- in picture form
- drawn in shapes or 'doodle' drawings
- in pen, pencil, coloured crayons or paint

Whatever form of 'writing' your prayer or prayers take, they need to have a meaning for you.

The epilogue

Reflective

What might the epilogue be to the parable of the prodigal son?

Did the family live happily ever after?

Did the younger and elder sons find a way of overcoming past hurts and become friends?

Did the younger son find happiness, embraced back into his family?

The prodigal

The Bible gives us no indication!

Yet, what stands out is not so much the jealousy of the elder son, or the recklessness of the younger, but the faith of the father/parent. This is someone who cares deeply, yet knows that it is not possible to control either son. This is the one who let the seeker go and discover. This is the one who is willing to risk loss through letting go. This is the one who offers unconditional love and forgiveness.

The forgiveness of the father/parent is not given in words but rather through action. Running, hugging, dressing and celebrating all speak louder than words of acceptance and forgiveness. Words are needed as well, but the action alone undeniably speaks the welcome home of the one who was lost, but now has been found.

- What has struck you most as you have worked with the story of the prodigal son?
- We do not know the epilogue to our own personal story, as it still has to be lived and experienced. What would you like that epilogue to include?

12–25 JUNE

Esther

Andrea Skevington

Introducing Esther

Bible reading

Esther is a strange, exotic book. It has the feel of Scheherazade's tales, full of powerful rulers and schemers, of danger and courage. Famously, it is one of two books of the Bible that do not mention God, and one of another pair that are named after women. It tells a story from the Exile, when Jewish people were taken as prisoners or slaves to the lands ruled by Babylon. It is clearly looking back, telling how the festival of Purim came to be. It does not mention the homeland or a longing to return; rather, it is a story of how people lived in an alien culture.

Structurally, it may remind its Jewish readers of the story of Joseph, with its setting in a powerful foreign court, and a sense of God's movement in events. The king's disturbed night is another connection. Joseph's story will remind us that exiles end and that good can be accomplished in the strangest ways.

Read through the whole book; take a few days if you need to. Ask God for openness. As you read, jot down anything you react strongly to—positive or negative. Keep a look out for words and phrases that snag your attention. Note them. Ask why, but don't rush to answers.

'God comes to you disguised as your life'
Paula D'Arcy, internet source

Reflective

Famously, the book of Esther contains no direct mention of God. It can allow us to interpret the story in the way we interpret our own lives—looking for signs of God, and love, and grace, in everything. Perhaps that is where we learn to find God, in the stuff of our lives.

This truth is expressed in what is perhaps the best-known verse in Esther: 'And who knows but that you have come to royal position for such a time as this?' (4:14, NIV 1984). There is a humility and a reverence in Mordecai's words—a sense that he is looking for purpose and meaning beyond earthly powers. Mordecai advises Esther on her next step, but neither of them knows what the outcome will be. Nevertheless, the step is to be taken.

Sometimes, we forget. Even if we are open to God as we read scripture, and pray, and worship, we may forget that all that comes to us can hint at the Giver. Our lives can speak to us of a God who is alive and active in many surprising ways.

This day, ask that you may be alive to the possibility that God is speaking to you and present with you in your life. Be alert, look out, ask questions of the events and people that come—what does this mean? What is there of love and grace in this? Is this person Jesus for me, someone I can serve today? (See Matthew 25:34–40; Luke 24:28–31.) Make today a day of active prayer as you are open to the possibilities God places before you. You might make a note of what you find.

The hidden God

Creative

I wonder if Mordecai and Esther felt part of a community that had been abandoned by God. The faith of Israel had become bound up with the land, and the system of temple worship.

Jeremiah wrote to the exiles (Jeremiah 29:4–23), telling them to settle down, make homes, pray and work for the good of the place where they were. He also warned them against prophets who spoke at this time. It is not surprising that Mordecai and Esther are reluctant to speak on God's behalf, or that they do not expect to hear from God. They are establishing their lives among their captors and living out the time of waiting.

Esther keeps her race and religion secret (2:10); nevertheless, events unfold to enable her to save her fellow Jews.

The festival of Purim, a celebration of that salvation, involves making and eating food where things are hidden—kreplach dumplings containing meat, for example. Masquerading is also the custom—part of the emphasis on disguise and the true nature of things being hidden. It is full of colour and surprises.

Two creative responses are suggested here: one of making and giving; the other of exploring your experience through visual art.

You could cook something for your family or friends, making something hidden—kreplach dumplings, a pie, biscuits with a surprise filling—and sharing it. Remember ways in which God has done surprising things in your life. Alternatively, you could bless someone with a surprise gift. You could hide a gift card for a coffee shop inside a gift for a homeless person, or a voucher or home-made card inside a book you loan or leave.

Or you may prefer to consider the title 'The Hidden God'. In what ways has God seemed hidden to you? How might you represent that visually? Can you think of a time when something good emerged from something bad? Give some time to allow ideas to form, and then paint or draw from that feeling or situation.

The golden sceptre

Bible reading

Power is an inescapable theme of this book—yet however absolute it seems, it has cracks. The king's power at the time stretched from India to Ethiopia and is laid out in the first sentence; the first chapter is a study in egotistic power play. The nobles and subjects are simply audience, and woman's beauty is degraded in this sordid charade. What matters is that the various appetites of the king are sated and that all dance to his tune.

The Old Testament is a collection of stories of the disempowered. It is the perspective of slaves, invaded peoples, younger sons and the defeated. Even in its brief glory under David and Solomon, Israel was not a mighty nation like this. The New Testament, too, gives us the perspective of the excluded and marginalised. Jesus is a servant king, so different from Xerxes.

It is easy to forget this as we look back at history through the lens of a powerful Christendom, with a powerful Church. It is easy to forget that God calls us to be a people under God's shepherding and that Jesus knelt at his followers' feet.

Consider some of the passages below, reflecting on any situations where you may be in a position of power—even in something as everyday as buying commodities.

- Ezekiel 34
- John 10:11–18
- Jeremiah 31
- Hebrews 8:10; 10:16
- 1 Samuel 8—9 (especially 8:6–9)

- Luke 20:46–47
- John 13:3–17

Are there ways you can honour and serve people in positions society may regard as inferior today? Can you bless people you normally overlook?

You could make some 'Thank you' or 'Bless you' cards to give to people you encounter.

Conflict

Reflective/creative

Esther's relationship with the king starts badly. We see how he treated his previous queen (1:10–20) and how women were regarded. We see how tyranny has its basis in fear, driving oppressive behaviour. The beauty pageant for a new queen must have been quite terrifying—to win would be a dangerous thing, to displease the king no better.

Esther and Mordecai follow a path of peace for as long as they can. They seem to be following the advice of Jeremiah to settle and make homes. They also seem to be acting in ways that foreshadow Jesus' teaching on living with powerful enemies—in his case, the Romans. They are living peaceably, and Mordecai assists the king, unjust as he is (2:19–23). Mordecai's reasons for not bowing down to Haman (3:1–5) are not made clear. Maybe Mordecai already saw Haman's character, or maybe this was one submission too far. However wise silence may seem, there are times when to bow feels like colluding. His refusal to bow is the catalyst that sets the rest of the plot in motion.

Consider a conflict situation you have been involved in or avoided. How far were you able to go along with things and where did you feel you had to take some kind of action? What was that?

How do you feel about it now?

Write or paint how you felt about the conflict, offering it to God. Offer forgiveness to yourself and others, or work towards being ready to do so.

Pray for the courage to be a peacemaker, and the wisdom to know how to take that positive course, as opposed to simple conflict avoidance.

You might like to explore this further by reading Martin Luther King's sermons *Strength to Love* or Desmond Tutu's *No Future without Forgiveness*.

Lament—the 'bitter cry'

Imaginative

Mordecai's refusal to bow provoked a terrible desire for revenge in Haman. His intention became to wipe out all the Jewish people within the empire. It is agreed with the detached pomp of despots— with signet rings and decrees. The king sits down to drink, while the city is thrown into confusion (3:15).

Mordecai does not feast; he mourns, and the rest of the people mourn with him (4:1–3). Esther's response to her uncle's grief is what most of us would do—she tries to make it right, to cheer him up, sending him clothes as if he wore sackcloth from poverty, not choice. Her distress is deep, and compounded by the difficulties in communication. Notice how hard it is for people to talk to each other, and to the king, in this story. Social structures deliberately isolate them, but they find a way to speak anyway. Esther's choice of Hathach as intermediary seems significant (4:5).

As you read this section of the story, imagine the feelings of Mordecai and Esther. Mordecai must feel the weight of his refusal to bow, the danger his people are now in. Esther, isolated from her community, relying on Hathach to know what is going on, must feel similarly. The closer she is to the seat of power, the more vulnerable she is.

Mordecai enters his people's rituals of lament. They express his heart.

Sometimes our faith can focus on joy to the extent that we do not know what to do with messy, tragic reality. Lament is a language we need. Lament is a powerful diagnostic of what is not right.

Read this section (3:1—4:5) imaginatively, putting yourself in the place of one who was in danger. Notice the response of the people—fasting, lamenting, sackcloth and ashes. Notice also how you feel as you encounter the danger. Talk to God about your experience and allow him the space to talk to you.

Consider a situation or an issue that you feel strongly about. Allow yourself to enter into the negative feelings. You might use one of the psalms or the book of Lamentations to give voice to your feelings (for example, Psalm 139 and Lamentations 1:1–5 express grief at the Exile, connecting with this story). Again, offer those feelings to God and ask him what you could do with them.

Courage

Intercession

Read Esther 4:7–17. Mordecai tells Esther to act, releasing her from his order not to say that she is a Jew. She is very aware of her vulnerability, her powerlessness. She suspects she is no longer the king's favourite (v. 11b). To keep her identity hidden up to now has been the sensible course, but the situation approaches crisis, and a different strategy is called for.

Mordecai's words in verses 12–14 begin with a stinging accusation that Esther is considering her own safety, not caring for the fate of her people. The words, perhaps unjust, shock her out of the paralysis of her powerlessness. I particularly like the words 'relief and deliverance for the Jews will arise from another place'. There is a confidence in this assertion, a deep faith in the saving power of God.

We see that Esther's courage is helped by the knowledge that she is not alone. She calls for the community to fast together, to prepare the way for her approach to the throne.

Are there ways you can develop solidarity in prayer with people facing difficulties? There may be people in your community, and those far away, who would value your support. If you can, pray with others.

Take time today to let someone know you are praying for them.

Perhaps you can also be a means of relief and deliverance for someone.

Such a time as this

Reflective

'And who knows but that you have come to royal position for such a time as this?'
ESTHER 4:14, NIV 1984

It is good to know that even in the most difficult, the most repressive of situations, God is at work. For that is the implication of Mordecai's words. He is hinting at the providence of God, always at work, always finding a way even when human power, greed and destruction seem overwhelming. I do not see any justification for the unjust use of power here, but I do see a call to action on behalf of the vulnerable: speaking up, taking a stand. We can learn from Mordecai and Esther in this situation. It is important to give courage to those in difficulties and it is important to discern when we may be the right person in the right place to make a difference.

Write down times when someone came into your life at just the right time, or said and did something that made a difference to you at a difficult time. Write out your feelings before and after the event. Notice how powerful even seemingly small gestures can be. As you do this, give thanks, and pray for the eyes to see when you can bless someone else in a similar way.

Now is the time

Creative

Take some time to contemplate 'such a time as this'.

Your current circumstances might be hard, or more straightforward. You may find yourself drawn towards thinking of these. Become aware that you are in the presence of God, who loves you. Your thoughts, and your times, are held in God's hands. As I wrote this, I remembered the exchange between Gandalf and Frodo in *The Fellowship of the Ring*:

> 'I wish it need not have happened in my time,' said Frodo.
> 'So do I,' said Gandalf, 'and so do all who live to see such times. But that is not for them to decide. All we have to decide is what to do with the time that is given us.'
> J.R.R. Tolkien

Alternatively, you may find yourself drawn to contemplating the 'now'—the present moment, becoming fully aware of your surroundings, all you can hear and feel and smell, the sensations within your own body, thoughts as they ebb and flow in your mind. You may remember that now is the only time we truly inhabit, and then begin to inhabit it more fully.

In response to either of these, you can draw, paint, write. You could make a *Carpe Diem* (seize the day) poster to put up by your bathroom mirror, for instance, or one with a favourite Bible verse.

You might wish to express what you are feeling at this point in your journey. A story or a poem might begin to emerge as you write.

Go with it, trusting the process, and see where it takes you.

Esther did not know the outcome of her actions and neither do we. We simply begin.

A wide table

Reflective

The book of Esther is structured around feasts.

There are the feasts of Xerxes at the beginning, where feasting is a display of fabulous wealth and power, a feast that feeds the king's ego (1:1—2:18).

Then there are the feasts of Esther, where she shares a table with her enemy and seeks to speak with the king when he has eaten and drunk. This feast is prepared for with fasting (2:19—7:10).

Finally there are the feasts of Purim, when the Jews had 'happiness and joy, gladness and honour' (8:16). These are a great celebration of their liberation from death (8—10).

The feasts of Esther are preceded by a three-day fast for all the Jews in Susa and for the women who waited on Esther. Perhaps three days was the time allocated to coincide with the dark phase of the moon, a time of searching and sadness. Afterwards, Esther seems sure about what she will do, and the account is written with an awareness of another force behind events.

It is a masterful example of 'soft power'. Esther approached the king cautiously, knowing both his power and his anger. She invited Haman, her enemy, honouring him. We see how Haman responds (5:9–14). The king is softened, perhaps flattered, by Esther's invitation and the feasting, but for Haman that honour plays into his inflated ego differently, and fans his hatred for Mordecai. The dynamic of the long night awake has echoes of the story of Joseph and Pharaoh. The reversal of Haman and Mordecai is almost complete.

The second feast sees Esther reveal herself as one threatened by Haman's plot. She does not say directly that she is a Jew. Interestingly, she simply speaks of the terrible consequences of Haman's action and the king's order. The king speaks as if this is all news to him. He has not considered the situation from another perspective (7:3–6). Esther is helping him see—and this leads to understanding and to change.

Read Matthew 5:43–48—love your enemies. Are there ways you can reach out and do good to people you disagree with, or those who have done you harm? Sharing a meal may be appropriate, but a gift of good food, or some other gesture, is worth considering. Just talking to people who have a different background and opinion from you is powerful.

When an American mosque was vandalised, the local synagogue invited the people to share their prayer space. It had a profound effect on both, and on the wider community.

Esther did not attempt to resolve the problem at once. She established relationship first. In the context of relationship, change is much more possible.

Deliverance

Meditative/creative

We have already noticed how the Bible often gives an account of the vanquished rather than the victors—the slaves rather than the masters. Part of this view is a dependence on God to rescue and redeem rather than relying on 'horses and chariots'. It is a particular perspective of the powerless. These themes occur again and again, preparing the way for the deliverance and rescue we find in Jesus. The Easter story, of betrayal, death and resurrection, is foreshadowed here. The joy of the Purim celebrations is a foretaste of the joy we find in the early Church.

Think of the 'happiness and joy, gladness and honour' recorded in Esther and how sorrow turned to gladness, and mourning into a holiday (9:22). Then spend some time meditating on the Easter story, how there, too, sorrow was turned to gladness.

The following passages may also be of help:

- Acts 2:42–47
- Ephesians 1:15–23
- Colossians 1:9–14

Express your thanksgiving. You may wish to use music, dancing, prayer, visual arts, or writing. Give time to giving thanks for your deliverance, your presence in the kingdom of light.

The final feast

Creative

The purpose of this book is to establish and perpetuate the festival of Purim (9:20–32). The people are commanded to eat, drink and make merry, according to the Talmud. *Shalak manos* (sending out portions) is the practice of sending gifts of food. These gifts are to others in the community and especially to the poor to ensure that they too can make merry.

Several times in the final chapters we read of how feasting and celebrations broke out as the news spread through the empire; a life-affirming response to the Jews' deliverance.

The date of Purim, usually held in March, will vary according to the Passover. If you have Jewish friends or acquaintances, you could ask them about Purim and what the book of Esther means to them.

As, for Christians, each Sunday is a mini celebration of Easter, it might be appropriate next Sunday to celebrate your deliverance from darkness to light, from death to life. Eating, drinking, merrymaking, or sending gifts of food to others, including perhaps a homeless person or a foodbank, could be part of your festival. You might wish to make things that pick up the 'God in disguise' theme.

It's time to celebrate!

26 JUNE–9 JULY

Peter

Sally Smith

Simon Peter

Introduction

I don't know about you, but I have a soft spot for Peter. He is the disciple I relate most easily to—maybe that says more about me than Peter? He's the one who jumps in with both feet and gets into a mess. He has all the best of intentions, but somehow it all seems to go wrong. He says and does the things I think I either would have done, or would like to have done had I had the courage to do so. He takes no half measures; if he's going to do something he does it fully and then considers the consequences. In modern, secular terms he would not be the first choice to have as a close follower or as the person to leave behind to continue your work. You can almost guarantee he will get something wrong and create a mess that needs to be cleared up. And yet Jesus chose him to be one of his closest followers and to be the rock on which the early Church would be built. Jesus also just kept on forgiving him, helping him pick himself up and carry on. How tolerant can I be of those who fail or mess things up? Maybe it was because he was forgiven again and again that Peter remained loyal to the end.

So who was Peter? His original name was probably Simeon, a Hebrew name changed to Simon by many Jews. He was the son of Jonah and had a brother called Andrew. He was born in Bethsaida (John 1:44) but he lived at some point in Capernaum in Galilee (Mark 1:21–31). He was married (1 Corinthians 9:5) and worked as a fisherman. His brother, Andrew, was a disciple of John the Baptist and it was likely that Peter was also affected by the movement following John's teaching.

Many of us know bits of the life of Peter, but we rarely put them all together. Before we begin you might like to pause and recall all you can about Peter. How many of his actions and adventures can you list? As we explore Peter's life notice if there are any surprises, stories you hadn't associated with him, or any omissions of your favourite events; inevitably there will be some things left out in such a short exploration.

The calling of Peter

Imaginative

We know from John (1:40) that Andrew was a follower of John the Baptist and that Andrew was then pointed towards Jesus, and he recognised in Jesus the Messiah, the anointed one.

Jesus is passing the boats and sees Simon and Andrew casting a net into the sea (Mark 1:16), and calls them to follow him and fish for people. Luke adds a miraculous catch of fish to the events.

Imagine the scene from Luke 5:1–11 (NRSV).

There are two boats, pulled up on to the shore. The owners and other fishermen are around them, cleaning and mending the nets. Listen to them as they work. Watch the skill in their mending. Feel the sun and smell the water. Maybe join in with them, or sit aside and watch. As you get to know them, work out which is the owner called Simon and which is his brother, Andrew.

A short distance away there is a large crowd of people. They seem to be pressing against one man. Watch and see if you can work out what is happening. What do they want from this man? How is he dealing with them? You recognise him as Jesus.

The crowd pushes so they start to get nearer to the fishermen. Watch as the men begin to realise that the people are approaching and they could possibly be in danger of being crushed.

Jesus turns to Simon and Andrew and asks if he can climb into their boat and go a little way out on to the water. Simon agrees and lets Jesus climb into his boat and manoeuvres it away from the shore. Jesus sits down and begins to talk. Listen to him and watch the crowd. See how Simon reacts. How does it feel to be listening to Jesus?

He turns and tells Simon and Andrew to put their nets over the side of the boat into the deep water for a catch. Simon protests. Listen as he explains that they have tried all night and not caught a thing, but watch as he gives in and agrees to give it a go. Is he enthusiastic or resigned? Then see how many fish they catch. You might go and help get the catch in.

As the boat begins to sink with the weight of the fish, Simon declares, 'Go away from me, Lord, for I am a sinful man!' Listen as Jesus replies: 'Do not be afraid; from now on you will be catching people.'

They haul the boat on to the shore and immediately follow Jesus.

Jesus turns to you. What do you say to him?

Are you prepared to follow as easily as Simon? What does he say to you?

Simon becomes Peter

Creative

According to John (1:42) it is at their first meeting that Jesus calls Simon 'Peter', an Aramaic word by which he was then known—often as Simon Peter. *Kepha* or *Cephas* is the Aramaic for 'rock' or 'stone'. In some of the epistles he is referred to as Cephas (for example, 1 Corinthians 1:12 and Galatians 2:9), though usually it appears in the Greek form of the word, *Petros*. Until this point Petros had not been used as a name.

For Peter this defined who he would become and his future role. Names are an important part of who we are. How do you feel about your name? What does it say about you? How well do you feel you fit your name?

Take a large sheet of paper and some coloured pens, crayons or pastels. Settle somewhere quiet and acknowledge you are in the presence of God, who calls you by your name.

Slowly, maybe even using your non-preferred hand, write your name in large, empty outlines of letters. If you have a long name you may want to use an abbreviation. Without thinking about what you are doing, fill in the letters with colours, patterns, shapes or pictures. Let the name dictate what you include. Don't judge the content or the quality of what you are doing. As you work, notice any reactions or feelings that emerge within you. Don't stop them or analyse them; just let them flow, and when they are ready, let them pass.

When you have finished, look at your name. Recall the feelings and thoughts that passed as you worked. You may want to make notes around the letters, reminding you of what was happening. As you explore your name, invite God to be alongside you, and listen to his wisdom on the person he is accompanying.

You are the Rock

Going out

While in Caesarea Philippi Jesus asks his disciples, 'Who do people say that the Son of Man is?', and then who *they* said he was (Matthew 16:13–18, NRSV). In response to Peter's reply, Jesus says, 'And I tell you, you are Peter, and on this rock I will build my church…' From Mark 3:16 we can guess that the name 'Peter' was given to Simon much earlier.

Go outside and find a large rock. Feel it. Feel how hard it is and how difficult to move. If you can, stand on it and feel it beneath your feet. Notice how stable it is. How does it feel to be standing on something so immovable? If you can't find a large rock, you could use concrete or a solid path.

As you stand, be aware of this rock as the foundation of the Church. What does it stand for? How does the Church allow this strong foundation to support it? How does this foundation enable the Church to serve God in the area where you live?

As you stand, ask that the stability of the rock on which the Church was built be part of your faith as well. Be aware of that foundation and all it gives, often unseen, to the world. How can you begin to relate to this foundation and draw on its strength?

You may like to take a small stone home with you as a reminder of the foundation of the Church and of your faith.

The keys of the kingdom

Creative/imaginative

As well as giving Simon a new name (Peter), Jesus gave him the keys of the kingdom. Keys are used rarely in the Bible, but when they are, they signify power—as in Revelation 1:18 or Isaiah 22:22. While he was on earth Jesus gave Peter the keys, giving him the power of the kingdom and authority over it.

Take a key. It may be a simple Yale-style key or a more complex one. It may be on its own or part of a bunch.

What does this key allow you to do? Who else has this power? (Who else holds this key?)

Over the years, keys have been widely used as a symbol for Peter. They show the ministry Jesus had planned for him and which he undertook after Jesus' death.

What would symbolise your ministry? You may immediately think of something—a Bible for preaching, a pack of felt pens for children's ministry, a mug for hospitality, a card for encouragement, a diary for administration… or you may need to wait, or ask for God's inspiration.

Take an object that represents how you serve Jesus.

This is both our gift to God and his gift to us, but today let's focus on this as God's gift to us.

As you hold your object, acknowledge it as a gift from God. Receive it as such. How does this change your perception of this ministry?

Picture what you do in this, noticing the breadth and depth of your work.

Then notice that God is beside you as you work. Stay with that image and allow him to support and encourage you as you work.

Remember him with you and imagine his continued presence with those you serve long after you have left.

Thank God for his gift of this ministry and for the opportunities he has given you through this work.

Next time you hold this object, remember, it was and is a gift from God. Allow that to go with you in your ministry.

Who do you say that I am?

Creative

Jesus asks his disciples who others said that he was, and then he asks, 'But who do you say that I am?' It is Peter who answers, 'You are the Messiah, the Son of the living God' (Matthew 16:15–16, NRSV). Jesus' response is that this must have been a revelation to Peter from God. Jesus himself had not made this explicit.

If Jesus were to ask you who you say that he is, what would be your reply? Begin with your gut response—the first few words that come into your head—and stay with that for a few minutes.

What would you now like to add to this response?

Talk to Jesus about who he is for you, and allow him to respond and to further reveal to you who he is.

You may end up with a well-structured answer, or with a greater awareness that you are unable to put into words. Whichever, accept it as from God and carry it with you over the next few days.

Peter—all or nothing

Imaginative

One of the images we have of Peter is of the man who is always the first to volunteer, to jump into action without thinking it through first. He does everything wholeheartedly and doesn't skimp on his dedication to Jesus. 'Look, we have left everything and followed you' (Matthew 19:27, NRSV). There are several examples of this in the Gospels. We read of him jumping out of the boat to walk on water in Matthew 14, and of him being desperate for Jesus to wash the whole of him in John 13, and cutting an ear off a slave of the high priest in Gethsemane in Matthew 26. It is Peter who asks how many times he needs to forgive if another member of the church sins against him, suggesting seven times, but being told 77 times (Matthew 18), and at the transfiguration it is Peter who wants to build three dwellings for Jesus, Moses and Elijah on the mountain (Matthew 17).

Take one of these events. Picture the surroundings. Use all your senses to set the scene. Don't worry about accuracy; just try to imagine being there and be open to God talking to you through your imagination.

See Peter and the others who are present. Notice where you are standing, or you may even imagine what it was like for Peter. Listen in to conversations between those present.

Let the scene unfold, watching and participating as appropriate.

Notice where you are standing and how you get involved in the action. How do you respond to Peter and his actions?

When the action is over, spend some time telling Jesus what you have experienced and asking what you could learn from Peter.

Healing at the Gate Beautiful

Imaginative

Peter was present on many occasions when Jesus healed, and we assume he would have been present when his mother-in-law was healed in Matthew 8. He was certainly present when Jairus' daughter was raised from the dead.

After Jesus' death and resurrection, Peter was very quickly involved in healing people himself. He is sent for when Dorcas dies in Acts 9, and prays for her as she also is raised from the dead. In Acts 3 he heals the lame man at the Gate Beautiful, an entrance to the temple where this man had been carried to beg for money from those entering the temple for prayer.

Imagine the scene. You are outside the temple, by one of the gates. It is approaching three o'clock in the afternoon and people are beginning to enter the temple for the daily prayers. You watch as a man is carried to the gate by his friends and they lower him to the ground. He begins begging from those who are entering the temple. Notice how people react to him and how he responds. He has been in the same place every day for many years. Some of those entering will know him well; others will be seeing him for the first time.

You then notice Peter and John approaching the temple, and the man holds out his hands, asking them for alms. Peter and John stop by the man and look at him intently. See his expression as they look and he holds out his hands for money. Peter says, 'Look at us.' Look. What do you see as you look at Peter and John?

Peter continues, 'I have no silver or gold, but what I have I give you; in the name of Jesus Christ of Nazareth, stand up and walk.' Peter takes him by the hand and as his feet and ankles grow stronger he is able to stand on his own. Watch as he enters the temple with Peter and John. As he gains strength he begins to dance and leap and praise God.

How do you feel at this? What do you do next? You might follow and join in the praise, or you might find a quiet corner to offer your thoughts and prayers to God, or you might walk away. Do what you need to do, without judging yourself, but being aware that God goes with you and hears your response.

Peter the leader

Reflective

From the moment of his calling, Peter is seen by Jesus as a leader of the future Church, and Jesus spends time preparing Peter for the future role he will take. He is accepted as such by the other disciples and is expected to take the lead; he is also seen by those beyond as a person who would know what Jesus was doing (Matthew 17:24). He is one of those taken up the mountain for the transfiguration, and Jesus calls him and two others to pray in the Garden of Gethsemane.

After the resurrection it is Peter who says he is going fishing, leading to the miraculous catch and the breakfast they share with Jesus on the beach and Jesus' command to Peter to feed his lambs.

It is therefore natural that at the beginning of Acts it is Peter who takes the lead in the appointment of a replacement for Judas and in preaching to the believers and later to the crowd with the coming of the Holy Spirit at Pentecost. He no longer has Jesus watching and supporting him directly, but he has been well prepared and is ready to take on the challenges before him.

It is not just the disciples who see him as the leader. He becomes the spokesman before the authorities and is seen by the community as being the one who has supernatural powers.

As we reflect back on the account of Peter we have in the Gospels, he is not the most likely candidate for leadership. I wonder how far he would get in modern selection processes? We sometimes have exacting requirements for our leaders, and our expectations can be greater than any human could fulfil. But from the moment they met, Jesus knew Peter had what would be needed. He would have seen the leadership he showed in his life as a fisherman and was able to see how that could be transferred into fishing for people. Peter would not at that point have understood what that was going to involve.

Spend some time considering people in your church who are maybe not using all their gifts and ask God how you could encourage them to consider being open to being used by God in new ways.

Then take those who are in positions of leadership and hold them before God, asking for a realistic view of their abilities and roles and asking the Holy Spirit to give to them as they need.

Peter the preacher

Creative

Once we start to read Acts we see Peter being used to preach to huge crowds, to proclaim the good news to all who would hear. He was obviously successful and open to being used by the Holy Spirit as hundreds began to follow Christ's teaching as delivered by Peter and the other disciples.

Peter is clear on what this good news is. Read his speech following the healing of the man at the Gate Beautiful in Acts 3:12–26.

This was a specific speech for a specific audience at a specific time, but it contains many truths we can follow as well.

Think of an individual or a group of people you spend time with. How would you tell them about Jesus? Where would you start? What do you think you would need to include and what would you leave out? Begin to write a speech for these people. Ask God for his guidance as you do so.

You may never get the opportunity to deliver this speech, or you may get an opportunity to slowly offer parts of it over time. Hold these people before God and ask him to give you the opportunities and the words you need when they arise.

Notice how you feel as you prepare, and hold those feelings and thoughts before God, allowing them to become your prayer.

Call to the Gentiles

Reflective

Peter is called to spread the message of Jesus to the Gentiles, to widen it beyond the Jews. He has a dream in which he is told that there is no longer unclean food and that he must be ready to meet with anyone he is sent to see. He is immediately invited to the house of Cornelius, which would have been an unclean act for a devout Jew. The Gentiles then receive the Holy Spirit and are invited to seek baptism. This work inevitably brings criticism on him.

Do you know of people who are tackling new areas and receiving criticism for their work, or who are not being supported as they need?

Are there practices you are holding on to that may no longer be appropriate? Things you do, or don't do, that could be changed?

Are there any people you feel it is not appropriate to tell about Jesus? Are there groups of people today we are avoiding?

Later life

Reflective/Bible reading

Peter was subsequently imprisoned, but his later life is difficult to trace.

We have inevitably left out many parts of Peter's life. Have there been any surprises for you as you have explored the life of Peter? Are there parts of his life which now make more sense, or areas that raise further questions?

You might like to look through the Gospels and Acts to see what else happened to him. Note any surprises or connections with the Peter you have come to know. How do you now feel about him?

You might also like to read his letters and see how these relate to the Peter you have come to know.

Tradition has it that Peter was crucified in Rome under Nero on an upside-down cross, not believing himself to be worthy of being put on a cross as Jesus was.

10–23 JULY

Walls and boundaries

Janet Lunt

Walls and boundaries

Introduction

Walls feature in a large way in our lives. They shape homes, rooms, workplaces and sacred buildings, offering protection, shelter, privacy and surfaces for decoration. Some are beautifully crafted, such as dry-stone walls or vertical gardens. Boundary walls or fences delineate ownership, and in the past many old cities were walled for protection. Down history, mighty defence walls have been constructed, such as the Great Wall of China, Hadrian's Wall in the north of England, and the Berlin Wall. In the Bible, some walls are pivotal in a storyline, like those in the battle of Jericho, or in Belshazzar's feasting hall where 'the writing on the wall' appeared; many are linked with Jerusalem, both the earthly and the heavenly.

Equally indispensable to us are metaphors connected with walls and the spaces they create. We use phrases like 'walls of silence' and 'without walls'. In the Bible we find many wall metaphors. Psalm 61 speaks of God being a strong tower; Jesus spoke of going to prepare a place in God's house of many rooms (John 14:2–3); in 1 Peter 2:5, Christians are living stones being built into a spiritual house. We are also told that unless the Lord builds, our efforts are in vain (Psalm 127).

Sit quietly with a Bible in a room where you like to pray: consider why you choose this walled space, and thank God for it. Read Matthew 6:5–7. There is something intimate about the advice of Jesus to pray in secret and be rewarded by God in secret. It speaks of the importance of a growing relationship. In Psalm 139:15, the phrase 'secret place' describes the womb where each person is conceived and develops, hidden from all except their Maker; and in the secret place deep inside each of us, seeds of creative ideas and love spring to life. Spend time with Jesus, in silence or response.

The Wailing Wall

Creative

Around the world there are many sacred places, often buildings set apart for worship or because something significant happened there. We know we can meet with God anywhere, yet some 'prayed-in' spaces seem to retain a special atmosphere of God's holiness and presence. In Old Testament times, the temple in Jerusalem was such a place and a destination for pilgrims—among them Jesus and his family. King Solomon acknowledged that the heavens could not contain God, let alone the First Temple he had built. Nevertheless, at its consecration, Solomon prayed, 'May your eyes be open towards this temple night and day, this place of which you said, "My Name shall be there"… Hear the supplication of your servant and of your people Israel when they pray towards this place. Hear from heaven, your dwelling place, and when you hear, forgive' (1 Kings 8:29–30).

Since the Diaspora, Judaism's most significant site is the Wailing Wall in the heart of Jerusalem—the western face of the Temple Mount and historic remains of the Second Temple. People of any faith are allowed to pray there by entering the appropriate fenced area. At dusk, spotlights enhance the huge golden blocks of stone where prayers written on scraps of folded paper can be seen tucked into the crevices. I visited the Wall, and was overwhelmed by the power of the place. I could imagine that visitors, inspired to greater faith, post prayers that dare to ask for more than usual, even for the deepest desires of their hearts.

Find pen and paper.

Consider what is the deepest, even secret prayer of your heart, maybe not yet voiced… Write your prayer down and fold it small.

Choose a special and secret place to put it, for example outside in a crack in a tree, a gap in a wall, under a stone; or indoors in a box, bowl or Bible. Add more written prayers during the next two weeks.

Priorities

Imaginative

It was Nebuchadnezzar II of ancient Babylon who destroyed Jerusalem and Solomon's Temple in around 587BC, taking the people of Judah captive to Babylon and commandeering temple objects to use for his own god. The Babylonian empire was later subsumed into Persia. When Cyrus became king of Persia, he respected the beliefs of the Jewish exiles in Babylon. He issued edicts permitting them to return to Jerusalem and to rebuild its temple, giving back all their temple artefacts. The story is told by Ezra and Nehemiah in the Old Testament. Both were men of prayer and Jewish officials who were involved in the Judean restoration: Ezra, a priest and scribe, was concerned with restoring the religious foundation of his people; Nehemiah was overseeing the repair of the broken city walls so the whole exiled community could return to live there, and he would become governor.

The book of Ezra informs us that the temple altar is constructed first, on the original spot, and that morning and evening sacrifices are offered straight away, according to Moses' law. After the foundations are laid, the priests, musicians and people who have returned to build gather to give thanks and praise to the Lord, amid tears of joy and reminiscence. Next the temple is built. Much later, due to lengthy hitches caused by Samaritan neighbours, the city walls are completed, after which the people gather to hear and commit themselves to the law and to dedicate the walls (Nehemiah 8). Both accounts describe the rebirth of God's community through an impressive order of priorities. Before any walls of protection are constructed, worship is restored, which is the beating heart of the people.

Read Ezra 3:10–13. Imagine yourself among the people returning from exile to Jerusalem, seeing its broken walls and temple ruin… help to clear rubble and work on building the altar… experience the emotional ceremony of thanksgiving with the sound of trumpets and cymbals… sense the rising hope and the beginning of healing.

What is the beating heart of all you do?

Respond to God with a suitable offering or sacrifice, for example of time, prayer or worship.

Problem walls

Creative

We loved the terraced Victorian house we lived in when our four children were small—its spacious rooms, and nice touches from skilled hands. We valued the sound-resistant walls that afforded the freedom to play recorders, trumpet and drum kit without the neighbours complaining.

The trouble with old houses is that they are prone to damp and rot. Our first experience of dry rot, affecting walls and woodwork, was quickly contained, demanding only that we move out overnight to avoid exposure to chemicals. Redecoration complete, guarantee in place, we relaxed back into normality. But within a year we spotted signs in the hall, too far from the original rot to fall within the guarantee. Radical treatment was required. The affected area included the passage separating the kitchen-diner from the rest of the house, where a chasm was created to expose foundations.

Everyday living became a feat, negotiating childproof barriers, and delivering food and drink via springy planks across the chasm. Stress levels rose. We couldn't have survived those weeks without the loving support of fellow Christians. They helped us reduce the bill by aiding with preparation and finishing work, and the brave invited the six of us for meals. The crowning experience came in the way only God can provide. With little time or energy for prayer during that period, I simply glanced at a book of daily verses for crumbs of sustenance. One very low day, I read:

> 'Can a mother forget her nursing child,
> or show no compassion for the child of her womb?
> Even these may forget,
> yet I will not forget you.
> See, I have inscribed you on the palms of my hands;
> your walls are continually before me.'
>
> ISAIAH 49:15–16, NRSV

Although the text refers to the walls of Jerusalem, its meaning was not lost. I took to heart that our heavenly Father was overseeing our plight. These timely verses provided great comfort, if not a little humour.

Take a sheet of paper and coloured pencils. Draw round your hand and let the outline represent God's hand. Draw and decorate your name within it, or colour freely, as you respond to being held in God's loving care and gaze.

Repairers and builders

Reflective

Read chapter 58 of Isaiah.

It seems that God's people wanted approval, but were following the letter rather than the spirit of the law. It had to be spelled out to them that ritual, fasting and sacrifice were meaningless, even offensive to God, without an accompanying inner transformation that would see them become repairers and restorers instead of abusers.

With good intentions, the self-discipline of fasting can help to sharpen our prayer, aiding us in the quest to become more like Christ. Yet in Isaiah 58 it can be quite daunting reading all God's requirements in order that our 'light will rise in the darkness'. Perhaps these requirements can be summed up in the words of Micah 6:8:

He has shown you, O mortal, what is good.
And what does the Lord require of you?
To act justly and to love mercy
and to walk humbly with your God.

These requirements are echoed in the Beatitudes of Jesus in Matthew 5: 'Blessed are the meek… those who hunger and thirst for righteousness… the merciful… the peacemakers…' Isaiah recounts several blessings that God's people can receive through living just, merciful and humble lives, some of which are below; verse 12b speaks expressly of the resulting benefits for others, even for whole communities.

- **v. 10b:** 'Your light will rise in the darkness, and your night will become like the noonday.'
- **v. 11:** 'The Lord will guide you always.'
- **v. 11:** 'The Lord will… satisfy your needs [in a sun-scorched land] and will strengthen your frame.'
- **v. 11:** 'You will be like a well-watered garden, like a spring whose waters never fail.'
- **v. 12b:** 'You will be called Repairer of Broken Walls, the Restorer

Walls and boundaries

of Streets with Dwellings.' (Or NRSV: '... repairer of the breach, the restorer of streets to live in.')

Reflect on the areas of mercy, humility and justice—in your heart and actions.

In what ways are you or could you (and perhaps your faith community) be a Repairer or Restorer of something broken, or a Builder of God's kingdom? Speak with God about new possibilities.

Glory within

Meditative

There are numerous images in the scriptures relating to boundaries which express God's love. For example, Jesus gave us the sheepfold analogy (John 10), revealing his loving protection. A vivid example is found in Zechariah 2:4–5: 'Jerusalem shall be inhabited like villages without walls, because of the multitude of people and animals in it. For I will be a wall of fire all around it, says the Lord, and I will be the glory within it' (NRSV).

Although Zechariah is referring to the city's rebuilding in Nehemiah's time, these verses demonstrate God's desire for those he loves. The metaphors of fire and glory can also be applied to the individual soul, the home or temple for God's indwelling. Settle in a relaxed but attentive position to meditate on this:

It is cold and dark outside. There is a knock on your door. It is the Lord! You welcome him over the threshold into the home of your soul.

He is carrying kindling firewood and a torch of fire. He has come to rekindle the fire in your hearth. You watch as he does this with care and expertise. Your dwelling glows again with warm, radiant light, which you welcome.

You invite the Lord to eat with you, and share what you have with him, however meagre. As you eat, you find your offering has been transformed into a feast.

You ask him about things that are on your heart.

He speaks to you about something on his heart.

When it is time for the Lord to leave, you thank him for sharing his glory with you.

You stand awhile in the open doorway, and notice that the firelight is radiating out of your windows and doorway into the darkness—a waymark for travellers.

You spend time in contemplation before the fire.

You may want to record something of your time with the Lord, adding it to your special place.

Neglect

Reflective

I never imagined that 13 years after our dry rot experiences we would face a much worse case. We had moved to a house that was not our own, and immediately my now-experienced eye spotted a sign of dry rot in a skirting board. But the landlord was neither worried nor interested. Two years later, the rot became obvious and widespread. The back half of the house—floors, lintels and walls—had been infected, the cause being a large fungus hidden in the foundations which fed on a leaking downpipe and fruited when the temperature was just right. The dry rot had crept up the walls behind plasterwork to reach the upper floor. Ten weeks of radical work were required. Furniture and carpets were stacked; at one point there was no kitchen sink, just a standpipe. Our youngest two, now teenagers, still lived at home and one slept in a bedroom with a gaping view of the dining room below; similarly, the bathroom lost its privacy. The piano filled with plaster dust. This time, the large-scale problems were due to a landlord's neglect, and we were more alone in our struggle, relieved only that we didn't need to meet the bill. Yet we survived, albeit with a few tears and a lot of hard work. I recognised how easy it is to procrastinate, ignoring responsibilities until there is a crisis, and realised how resilient we were becoming.

The dry rot fungus, hidden in the foundations, reminded me that sometimes we need to deal with ugly things that have taken root in dark corners of the soul, that show only when the temperature changes. Read Hebrews 12:15. Spend time prayerfully checking for any unforgiveness or irritation that could fester and take root in your soul, bringing anything you find to Jesus for cleansing and healing.

Prayerfully consider if you are putting off something that could be done sooner or even today, to avoid missing the moment or neglecting an opportunity to bless others.

Escape

Imaginative

Imagine the scene:

I have been arrested and taken to a prison cell, for doing nothing other than speaking about Jesus. I am to be tried in public, which no doubt means the crowds will side with the king. I expect the worst. Meanwhile, I am shackled to two soldiers; two more stand guard outside the door and, if that isn't enough, I am bound with chains. It's as if I am a murderer; but then, Jesus was treated like this. I sit on a damp, earth floor with my back against a cold stone wall. It is late; I'm exhausted from the rough handling of soldiers. I fall asleep.

Suddenly, I am nudged, poked. Is it time for the trial already? I wonder, not quite awake. I open my eyes to find an angel standing in front of me! Yes, definitely an angel, for the cell is brightly lit. It must be a vision. I must concentrate and listen.

The angel instructs me to get up, quickly. I obey, and instantly my shackles fall away! I must dress, disguise myself in my cloak and follow him. I do this hastily, and the angel leads me out of the cell. The soldiers inside and outside the room notice nothing—they are sleeping. It is dark outside as we exit the prison and head towards the gate of iron that leads into the city. The gate swings open of its own accord.

The angel leads me along a street. He stops, turns and gestures me onward, then… he is gone. Suddenly I am aware it has not been a vision or dream at all. Here I stand, with bruised wrists and ankles, freed of my chains and oppressive walls.

Based on Peter's imprisonment by Herod (Acts 12)

David composed Psalm 18 when the Lord rescued him from his enemies and King Saul. Sections of this psalm could have been a suitable response from Peter.

Freedom comes in many forms. Use Psalm 18:1–6, 16–29 as a prayer and tribute to God who sets his servants free. Write out a verse that strikes you and keep it in your special place.

Walls of separation

Intercession/liturgy

After World War II, Germany and Berlin were divided between East and West. Soviet-controlled East Germany built the Berlin Wall in 1961 to keep the West out permanently, maintaining the division with armed guards who shot on sight anyone seen trying to escape to the West. Many families were split apart. In November 1989, peaceful demonstrations finally pressurised East Berlin's government to cease hostilities and allow open access. Television news showed the moment when the first graffiti-covered section fell. The wall, a powerful symbol of control and division, was being dismantled before our eyes, and I imagined the risen Jesus striding through the breach.

Another separating wall, the Israeli West Bank Barrier, is still under construction and will eventually be over 400 miles long. It adds new disputes and hardship to the tense relationship between Israel and Palestine. The wall artist Banksy, as famous for anonymity as for political street art, has created nine thought-provoking images on the Palestinian side of the wall in peaceful protest (search for images online: Banksy in Palestine): a little girl is lifted to the top by helium balloons; a young child frisks an Israeli soldier; scenes of beauty are viewed as if through apparent breaches; a bunch of flowers is aimed over the wall by an archetypal fire-bomber. Banksy believes that the wall 'essentially turns Palestine into the world's largest open prison', although the number of suicide bombings against Israel has decreased as a result of the wall.

Read Ephesians 2:13–16 and pray for peace in our divided world.

For Palestine and Israel

**Christ Jesus, our peace,
destroy the wall of hatred that divides.**

For countries with tyrannical regimes or under attack

**Christ Jesus, our peace,
destroy the wall of hatred that divides.**

*For peace between religions,
and divisions within the Christian Church*

**Christ Jesus, our peace,
destroy the wall of hatred that divides.**

For divided families

**Christ Jesus, our peace,
destroy the wall of hatred that divides.**

For refugees

Christ Jesus, hear these prayers; destroy the walls of hatred that divide, make opposing groups one through your cross and be their lasting peace.

Amen

The Selfish Giant

Story

We are all capable of building walls, often out of fear rather than need. Some boundaries, physical and metaphorical, are necessary, but some prevent relationship—sometimes keeping Christ out of our life.

There are several stories about building and destroying walls.

Read Oscar Wilde's short story 'The Selfish Giant' (in the public domain: available in libraries or online at www.eastoftheweb.com/short-stories) or another similar story.

Down but not destroyed

Creative/reflective

We live in a modern house now, with no children left at home; they visit us with their children. Recently we experienced a new 'wall' situation, due to years of neglect of a different landlord. A large section of an old stone boundary wall, separating our garden from a graveyard, fell in, finally weakened by winter. Fortunately, no one was hurt. The view from our sitting room became one of graves, a public footpath and piles of large stones through which tenacious weeds grew. We lost our privacy and felt vulnerable at night. We had to face 18 months of deliberations.

Sadly, the fall flattened and covered three six-foot shrubs. Just the bare tips of one, a flowering currant, peeped beyond the rubble. I identified deeply with these bushes because a painful life situation was also happening to me. Yet, weeks later, I noticed tiny new buds had appeared on the few visible tips of the one bush. This miracle of nature kick-started me into hope-filled action—on went the gardening gloves as I set about rescuing the shrub. Although I couldn't lift the heavy coping stones, I rolled some of them aside and succeeded in propping the plant upright with the same stones. Soon the battered shrub burst into glorious flower. A friend shared her thoughts with me, saying that although heavy things can fall on us in life and sometimes nearly crush us, God's life within is not destroyed; Jesus gives living water that wells up to eternal life, so there is always fresh water for the soul. Her words and the gift of the flowering bush watered my flagging soul.

Fill a glass with fresh, preferably sparkling water. Place it in front of you.

Read 2 Corinthians 4:6–11, 16–18. Wonder at being a vulnerable earthen vessel in which God's transcendent glory can be seen. Reflect on times when you have been aware of 'living water' filling you and spilling over to others.

If God's life in you has been rejected by anyone, be encouraged by St Paul's experiences. Speak with God about things that weigh you down.

When you are ready, drink from your glass of water, asking to be filled afresh with the 'living water' that Jesus offers.

Gateways to heaven

Bible reading/creative

In my youth, I imagined heaven as a jewelled city, long before I knew of the description in Revelation 21. Images were imbibed through singing hymns that spoke of gates of pearly splendour and crowns cast around the glassy sea, among others, and a gospel song told of twelve gates into a beautiful city.

Read Revelation 21:10–26.

This whole chapter from Revelation paints a striking picture of the New Jerusalem, symbolically portraying a safe place where riches and healing, refreshment and God himself are available to all its inhabitants. The entire city, its cubic design akin to the past 'holy of holies', is itself filled with God's presence and glory. The city walls imply security, while the ever-open pearl gates could represent welcome and freedom. It is thought that the precious gems symbolise perfection. A similar but shorter vision appears in Isaiah 54:11–14, and Isaiah 60:18 adds an interesting metaphor that God's people will call their walls Salvation and their gates Praise.

However, this may not be how you desire heaven to be. Some Christians imagine green pastures, a far-off shore across the river of death, or a paradise garden like Eden restored. Others major on freedom from pain, and rest or joy, rather than on anything visual. Whatever the future will be like, we can all echo the words of 1 Corinthians 13:12: 'For now we see only a reflection as in a mirror; then we shall see face to face. Now I know in part; then I shall know fully, even as I am fully known.'

In *The Complete Bible Handbook* (Dorling Kindersley, 2004), John Bowker writes that Revelation's 'kaleidoscopic visions have an effect more like music than as logical argument'. In turn, perhaps the invisible mystery we call music can help us to *feel* what eternity with God is like, instead of trying to visualise it.

How do you imagine heaven to be?

Listen to a piece of recorded music (or revisit a hymn or song) that you would describe as heavenly. As you do this, rest in the presence of the Eternal One who, one day, you will fully know.

Using the metaphor of walls and borders, have a go at completing the following sentence:

'God is like a house/garden/vineyard/city/tower/(other) in whose walls I…'

24 JULY–6 AUGUST

Beside the sea

Dorinda Miller

B for beach

Introduction

Summer and seaside are, in my mind, as closely connected as fish and chips and bucket and spade! Growing up in the south of England, the journey to the seaside only took an hour and we would frequently go for day trips in the summer. So, given that we are now in the season of summer, our theme for the next fortnight will be BESIDE THE SEA. We will look at this by taking a theme for each letter of the phrase: B for beach, E for encourage, S for sea, I for insight, D for drown, E for enjoyment, T for tired, H for harbour, E for exit, S for sky, E for everywhere, and A for always.

You may be familiar with the music-hall song that John Glover-Kind wrote in 1907, 'I do like to be beside the seaside'. It expresses the singer's love of the seaside and his desire to return there each year for his summer holidays. The lyrics of the chorus are:

> *Oh! I do like to be beside the seaside*
> *I do like to be beside the sea!*
> *I do like to stroll along the prom, prom, prom*
> *Where the brass bands play:*
> *'Tiddely-om-pom-pom!'*
> *So just let me be beside the seaside*
> *I'll be beside myself with glee*
> *Beside the seaside!*
> *Beside the sea!*

How do these sentiments resonate with you? Take a few moments to reflect on the following:

- What have you enjoyed and relished about being on the beach beside the sea?
- Is there anything that you dislike about being on the beach beside the sea?
- How have you encountered God on the beach beside the sea?

You may like to record your reflections in your journal and then use them in a time of praise and thanksgiving for all you have enjoyed and received from God while being beside the sea.

E for encourage

Bible reading

'Encourage' appears in the Bible between 14 and 92 times— depending on which version you read! Whatever our individual age or stage of life, receiving and giving encouragement is beneficial to us all, whether this be in general terms, or more specifically in our faith.

So let's begin by reminding ourselves of some of the verses which mention 'encourage' in the New Testament (NIV).

In Romans 12:8, Paul lists encouragement as a gift of the spirit. 'If it is to encourage, then give encouragement.'

In 2 Corinthians 13:11, Paul encourages the Corinthians to rejoice and to encourage one another. 'Finally, brothers and sisters, rejoice! Strive for full restoration, encourage one another, be of one mind, live in peace. And the God of love and peace will be with you.'

In 1 Thessalonians 5:11, Paul encourages the Thessalonians to continue encouraging each other. 'Therefore encourage one another and build each other up, just as in fact you are doing.'

In Hebrews 10:24, the writer of this letter urges the Hebrews to be creative in encouraging one another. 'Let's see how inventive we can be in encouraging love and helping out, not avoiding worshiping together as some do but spurring each other on, especially as we see the big Day approaching' (MSG).

Reflect now on times when people have encouraged you: how did they do so? How did it help you?

As you consider those times, ask God who he would have you encourage in this season and what you could do or say to encourage them.

Finally remember what Paul wrote to the Corinthians and be encouraged!

> *'God of all healing counsel! He comes alongside us when we go through hard times, and before you know it, he brings us alongside someone else who is going through hard times so that we can be there for that person just as God was there for us.'*
> 2 CORINTHIANS 1:4, MSG

S for sea

Imaginative

We will experience today's theme of the sea through an imaginative exercise and a reflection using a picture of the sea. You can use an image of the sea from the internet if you do not have one of your own to hand.

I would like you to imagine that you are on an empty beach. As you walk along the beach, take in as many details as possible. Feel the sea breeze and enjoy the warmth of the sun. As you walk, you notice that there is a wooden jetty going out into the sea. As you reach it, you decide to walk along it. When you get to the end, you notice that a boat is tied up and anchored. It is gently bobbing about in the sea.

I invite you to place in the boat all those people and situations that you are currently concerned about. Place them in the boat, one by one.

As you place the last one in, you hear footsteps coming up behind you. You turn and see an elderly man. He is the owner of the boat and he offers to take what you have placed in the boat for a boat ride, so that you are free to rest and enjoy the sun, sea and sound of the waves lapping against the jetty.

He gives you a chair and you sit down on it.

Before he gets into the boat, do you want to say anything to him and does he have any words of wisdom for you?

He gets into the boat and sets off. You watch him, until the boat goes round the headland and out of sight.

You sit and rest and enjoy the sun, sea and sound of the waves lapping against the jetty.

Now pick up your picture or look at it on the screen.

Look carefully at it. Notice the location, the weather, the time of day.

Notice as many details as you can. As you look, ask God what he wants to highlight to you through this picture. Take your time.

Now place yourself in the location. What feelings or thoughts emerge as you engage with the scene? What is God saying to you?

Ask God for a verse and let his words take you deeper into silence with him.

Now spend a few moments in praise and thanksgiving for what you have received from God during your time of reflection with this picture.

I for insight

Creative

Taking time out from our regular routine, whether it be a weekend, a week or longer, gives us the opportunity not only for rest and refreshment, but also for recall and reflection. A change of scene can bring us new insights, new experiences, new friendships, and it can allow us to consider new possibilities. These in turn can provide us with inspiration and motivation to return home with renewed energy and enthusiasm for our roles and responsibilities.

Read the verses below from Psalm 119 slowly three times and choose a word or phrase or sentence that strikes you or speaks to you. Ponder it for a few minutes.

Take a piece of paper, draw round a dinner plate and cut out the circle. You can then write out your chosen word/phrase/sentence, starting at the outer edge of the circle and writing it repeatedly, in decreasing circles, until you reach the centre. Turn it over and over in your mind and see what insights God shows you through it.

'God, teach me lessons for living
so I can stay the course.
Give me insight so I can do what you tell me—
my whole life one long, obedient response.
Guide me down the road of your commandments;
I love travelling this freeway!
Give me a bent for your words of wisdom,
and not for piling up loot.
Divert my eyes from toys and trinkets,
invigorate me on the pilgrim way.
Affirm your promises to me—
promises made to all who fear you.
Deflect the harsh words of my critics—

> *but what you say is always so good.*
> *See how hungry I am for your counsel;*
> *preserve my life through your righteous ways!'*
>
> PSALM 119:33–40, MSG

When you have finished, be thankful for the insights you have received and record them in your journal.

D for drown

Imaginative

Read Matthew 8:23–27.

Imagine that you are with the disciples and Jesus in the boat. Take time to survey the scene. What is the boat like? What is the weather like? What are the disciples discussing together? Where is Jesus? Whereabouts in the boat are you?

Suddenly the weather begins to change. The mood of the disciples changes. What are they saying, doing, feeling? How do you feel? What do you do?

The waves break over the boat. Which disciple wakes Jesus? Watch as Jesus stands and rebukes the wind and raging waters—they subside at his command.

How do you feel as Jesus says, 'Why are you afraid? You have so little faith!' Take a moment to consider your life at the moment. Is it stormy or calm? How do you respond to Jesus' comment about faith?

As the disciples look at each other and Jesus in fear and amazement, Jesus looks at you. What do you want to say to him? What does he say to you? Spend time listening to him as the boat sails calmly on and reaches the shore.

You all disembark. Watch as Jesus and the disciples walk together along the shore and into the distance.

Record your response to this meditation in your journal. Then spend a few minutes in praise and thanksgiving for how the Lord met you through it.

E for enjoyment

Reflective

'There is a time for everything, and a season for every activity under the heavens' (Ecclesiastes 3:1), and the Mars Bar strapline used to state that 'A Mars a day helps you work, rest and play'. The summer is a time for many of us to have a break from work and time to rest and play!

Paul, in one of his letters to Timothy, writes, 'Hope in God, who richly provides us with everything for our enjoyment' (1 Timothy 6:17). The writer of Ecclesiastes also makes various comments about enjoying life: 'So I commend the enjoyment of life, because there is nothing better for a person under the sun than to eat and drink and be glad. Then joy will accompany them in their toil all the days of the life God has given him under the sun' (8:15).

Take a few minutes to reflect on what gives you enjoyment by taking a piece of paper and drawing two buckets. On one write the ways you currently give out, for example through family, friends, work, church or community. On the other write the ways in which you currently take in, for example through exercise, creative activities, cultural activities, relationships and retreats. You may find that some activities fit in both buckets!

- Is there balance between these buckets or is one fuller than the other?
- Are there changes you need to make to achieve a balance which will be more life-giving for you and increase your level of well-being?

- Lay all of this before the Lord and, in the silence, listen to what he has to say to you. Thank him for what he has revealed to you.

Then take steps to ensure that you have time to participate in activities and events that are enjoyable and life-giving for you!

T for tired

Imaginative

We all have experience of feeling tired and weary. Sometimes in the days preceding a holiday, we are so busy preparing to go that when we arrive at our destination we can spend the first few days feeling increasingly tired and weary as we unwind from all that we have been experiencing in recent weeks or months. However, for some the saying 'A change is as good as a rest' proves to be the case, and the energy that comes from being somewhere different, with a different pace and opportunities to explore, can be invigorating.

However you are feeling today, I would like to invite you to consider the topic of tiredness through the following reflection.

Weary? Worn out? Exhausted? Dead beat? Sleepy? Drowsy?

These are just some of the words that spring to mind to describe feeling tired. There are many types of tiredness and different causes for it, for example physical tiredness, emotional tiredness and spiritual tiredness.

- Think for a moment about what causes you to be physically tired.
- Now consider what makes you emotionally tired.
- And now ponder what makes you spiritually tired.
- In the busyness of life, how aware are you of these types of tiredness, and what strategies have you developed and put in place to manage them?

- What are the barriers that arise to block these strategies?
- What are the benefits of persevering with them?

Imagine now that you are sitting in a comfortable chair and relaxing. Jesus comes and stands beside you. What would you like to say to him about feeling tired? What advice and encouragement does he give you?

Close this time of reflection by reading Isaiah 40:28–31 (NIV).

H for harbour

Reflective

As we sail over the sea of life, we soon learn that it is not all plain sailing! We encounter storms, turbulence and a variety of other conditions. Some are challenging, some are life-changing, some are life-giving. But none of them are unknown to God or beyond his reach, for he is everywhere. If you can, read Psalm 107:23–32 from *The Message* (available at www.biblegateway.com).

Just as boats and ships need harbours where they can moor safely in a sheltered port, so we too need time and places where we can go to rest and recover after traversing choppy waters.

Read the verses from Psalm 107 again and think of a time when you encountered a 'storm'. What was it? What happened? Where did you go? How did you manage in the circumstances? How did God meet you in the midst of the storm and what did you learn about yourself, others and God through it? Then take time to thank and praise God for his provision for you.

You may like to close by listening to the song 'Oceans (Where feet may fail)' which features on the *United* album by Hillsong. It is available on YouTube.

E for exit

Going out

The dictionary informs us that, as a verb, 'exit' means to go away or out; to depart or to leave. Leaving the dark evenings and the colder weather behind us, the season of summer gives us more opportunities to be outside. The warmer weather and lighter evenings provide scope for outdoor activities, and many of us take holidays during this season.

Spending time outdoors is beneficial. It can boost our creativity and focus, improve our mood and self-esteem, increase levels of vitamin D; and it allows us to connect with our creator.

'Nature is fuel for the soul,' said Richard Ryan, lead author of a study reported in the *Journal of Environmental Psychology* in 2010. He also commented that the study showed that connecting with nature was a better way to feel energised than having another cup of coffee!

God speaks through his creation, if only we will take the time out of our busy lifestyles and walk in the countryside. So I would like to encourage you to go to gardens, parks, the countryside, the seaside, and to look at the flowers, shrubs, trees, the sky and the clouds, the sand, rocks and sea.

Take time to simply 'be'. Take time to 'look' and see what is all around you. Take time to stop, to be still and to absorb the sights, smells, sounds of creation. Listen to what the creator wants to communicate to you through creation.

Record your reflections from outdoors in your journal and close by reading Psalm 148.

S for sky

Meditative

In the midst of our busy everyday lives we probably have little time to stop and gaze at the creation around us and the skies above us, although we may be struck by a beautiful sunrise, or sunset, or maybe even stormy skies or a rainbow. Today is an opportunity to stop and reflect on the sky through the following meditation.

Find a quiet place, sit in an upright position with your feet firmly on the floor and take a deep breath in and then let it out slowly. Do this a few times. Gradually let go of any tension or stress you may be feeling and become still and at peace.

What thoughts or images or memories spring to your mind when you hear the word 'sky'?

What sky-related phrases come to mind?

Recall now any times in your life when you have been aware of God's presence as you have looked at the sky, or times when you have looked at pictures or photos of the sky.

- What was it that God showed you through looking at the sky?
- What impact did it have on you?
- How did you respond?
- As you remember it now, how do you feel?
- Is there anything else that God wants to show you as you remember this specific time?

What is the sky like where you are today?

Take a moment or two to observe it and to consider what God might want to communicate to you through it.

Draw this time of meditation to a close by reading Psalm 147:5–8.

E for everywhere

Creative

The idea of being everywhere and nowhere was expressed in a song by Slade in 1985, and our pace of life may, at times, cause us to resonate with this! While we may find ourselves in a season of increased activity, or challenge or stress, with little time for reflection and less awareness of God's presence, this does not, in any way, diminish his presence with us.

He is everywhere, as the writer of Psalm 139 wrote:

> *Is there anyplace I can go to avoid your Spirit? to be out of your sight?… You'd find me in a minute—you're already there waiting!*
>
> vv. 7, 10, MSG

This was Jacob's experience when he was fleeing to his uncle Laban after he had received Isaac's blessing through deception (Genesis 27—28). He stopped for the night at Bethel on his journey to Haran, and while he slept the Lord appeared to him in a dream. In the dream he saw a stairway reaching from earth to heaven with angels going up and down it. The Lord was at the top. He spoke to Jacob about his descendants and the land, and promised that he would be with him wherever he went. 'When Jacob awoke from his sleep, he thought, "Surely the Lord is in this place, and I was not aware of it"' (28:16). His response to the dream was to take the stone he had used as a pillow and stand it up as a memorial pillar.

Reflect back over the past year and recall the times that you have, like Jacob, encountered God unexpectedly. Then, as an act of praise and thanksgiving, imagine building a small tower with bricks, where each brick represents an encounter. Or you may prefer to take a piece of paper and draw a tower and write on each brick, or build a tower with bricks if you have them available.

A recent example of God being everywhere is described in Mark Batterson's book *Draw the Circle: The 40-day prayer challenge* (Day 39, pp. 217–18). Ken Gaub was driving in Ohio, USA, and stopped at a restaurant. While his family went in, he took a few minutes to stretch his legs. He heard a payphone at the garage nearby ringing and ringing, so thinking it might be an emergency he answered it. The operator said she had a long distance call for Ken Gaub! He almost fainted—he was in the middle of nowhere! It transpired that a girl in Pennsylvania, USA, was contemplating suicide and decided to pray one more time. She remembered Ken from the television and thought he might help her. As she prayed, some numbers came into her head and she decided to dial them, and found herself speaking to Ken!

A for always

Reflective

In a fast-paced and swiftly changing world, it is reassuring to know that there are some elements that are always the same. The Bible tells us that 'As long as the earth endures, seedtime and harvest, cold and heat, summer and winter, day and night will never cease' (Genesis 8:22) and also that 'God, who is enthroned from of old… does not change' (Psalm 55:19). Furthermore, 'Jesus doesn't change—yesterday, today, tomorrow, he's always totally himself' (Hebrews 13:8, MSG).

As this series draws to a close, spend time with some verses from the book of Psalms. Choose one and turn your chosen verse over and over in your mind and see what God reveals to you through it. You may like to take it with you into your day and to repeat it at intervals during the day.

Beside the sea

*For I have always been mindful of your unfailing love
and have lived in reliance on your faithfulness.*
PSALM 26:3

*Look to the Lord and his strength;
seek his face always.*
PSALM 105:4

*Be my rock of refuge,
to which I can always go;
give the command to save me,
for you are my rock and my fortress.*
PSALM 71:3

*As for me, I shall always have hope;
I will praise you more and more.*
PSALM 71:14

Recall the key insights from your time 'beside the sea' and consider how these will impact your journey of faith. Then take time to praise and thank God for the ways he has revealed himself to you, and for his provision for you.

7–20 AUGUST

The wisdom of God in creation

Lisa Cherrett

Introduction

Proverbs is one of the Bible's Wisdom books, full of practical advice for a fulfilling and godly life. Most of it is written in the voice of a man, perhaps a father speaking to his son, but in chapter 8 a woman speaks—one called Wisdom. Verses 22–31, after listing many of Wisdom's attractive qualities, tell us something quite stupendous. Wisdom—not angels or the universe—was the very first thing created by God.

> 'The Lord brought me forth as the first of his works,
> before his deeds of old;
> I was formed long ages ago,
> at the very beginning, when the world came to be…
> I was filled with delight day by day,
> rejoicing always in his presence,
> rejoicing in his whole world
> and delighting in the human race.'
>
> PROVERBS 8:22–23, 30–31

It may be that the person named Wisdom by the writer of Proverbs 8 is the very same as the 'beautiful laws of physics' that, according to Professor Brian Cox, underpin the universe and the world we see around us. We might also identify her with the Holy Spirit hovering over the waters at creation in Genesis 1:2. However we imagine her, this first companion and helper of God is sheer joy—rejoicing, delighting or, as we might say, 'buzzing' with excitement over the vibrant creation of God, from oceans to mountains to green fields to man and woman in perfect unity.

The wisdom of God is both revealed and (as we shall see) hidden in the created world. In it we see various aspects of God's character, intelligence and practical skill as the creator of and provider for this world. We learn from the world about the things he delights and rejoices in, and we find that some of these characteristics are part of our human nature too, made in his image.

Be prepared to observe the created world more closely as we explore this theme. Pray as you get ready to delve into the wisdom of God in creation:

Creator God, Lord of heaven and earth, we are your children, made in your image, and you delight in us. Please show me more of your wisdom in creation—the principles that reveal to us your designs for the world. Awaken my creativity, and show me how to develop it in line with your wisdom.
Amen

Frameworks and boundaries

Bible reading

When the Old Testament writers consider God's work as a wise creator, their first thought is often about the way he establishes frameworks and boundaries, giving structure and purpose to the created world. So, in Genesis 1, light and darkness, day and night, sky, oceans and land are shown to be the basic framework of his creation. Then the spaces are filled with a profusion of plants, birds, sea creatures and land animals, each with their assigned habitats. The inclusion of sun, moon and stars allows for the repeated

The wisdom of God in creation

patterns of sleep and activity, the turning of the seasons, planting and reaping. By these rhythms and patterns a secure structure is put in place for the welfare of all living things.

When Wisdom speaks in Proverbs 8, she tells us specifically that God 'gave the sea its boundary' (v. 29). Psalm 104:9 says the same, and Job 38:8–11 shows us the 'fixed limits' of the sea, trapped by God behind 'doors and bars'.

It's interesting to note all the measuring and fixing words in these Bible passages. God challenges Job, 'Where were you when I laid the earth's foundation?' (Job 38:4). 'Who marked off its dimensions?... Who stretched a measuring line across it? On what were its footings set, or who laid its cornerstone?' (vv. 5–6).

Again, in Proverbs 8:27–29, God 'marked out the horizon on the face of the deep... and fixed securely the fountains of the deep... he marked out the foundations of the earth'. Try doing an online Bible search for 'marked' or 'measured' (www.biblegateway.com would be helpful). You'll find the same images repeated elsewhere in the Old Testament.

There is a vivid picture here of God the architect or builder, with a toolbox full of measuring rods, set square, spirit level, hammer and nails—and a well-sharpened pencil behind his ear. Perhaps it was no accident that his Son, Jesus (present with Wisdom at creation, according to John 1:2), grew up to be a carpenter/builder, bringing all that delight in measuring, marking and fixing right down to earth in a Middle Eastern village.

Measuring skill

Creative

The picture of God with his toolbox of measuring and fixing equipment is one that we will find easy to understand. It's a point of connection between us in our technologically advanced 21st century and the ancient writers of the Old Testament, far removed from us in time and culture. We know the saying 'Measure twice, cut once', and we can all grasp the wisdom required to make things that are fit for purpose, useful and beautiful. Some of us will have learned the principle by trial and many errors, whether we were making a cardboard crown to fit a child's head in Sunday school, hanging wallpaper, making curtains or engineering parts for a machine.

Are you a maker of any kind? Are you a dressmaker or tailor, a woodturner or metalworker, a potter, builder, designer or DIY enthusiast? Any and every occupation or hobby that requires some form of measurement or work with boundaries reflects God's wisdom in creation, and the joy and satisfaction it brings us is a clear sign that we are made in his image (Genesis 1:26).

What is your latest creative project? Perhaps you could do some further work on it today, reflecting on the way you are replicating, on a small human scale, the work of God in creation. You may not think you are practically gifted in this way. To do something really simple, you could find a ruler, mark some dots at regular intervals up and down a piece of paper, join up the dots to make squares or rectangles and then colour in the spaces to make a pleasing pattern. As you work, be aware of joining in God's work of creation. Work alongside the master creator.

If all else fails, take a walk around your home or up and down your street outside, and notice the many examples of human handiwork around you that have required skill in measuring, marking out or fixing in place. Thank God for this skill in other people.

Awe and wonder

Going out

We may understand the principle of careful measurement and

The wisdom of God in creation

secure fixings, but this doesn't mean that God's creation is on a scale that we can easily grasp or that it is designed solely with us in view. This is the message, spoken loud and clear, of Job 38—39. Light and darkness, thunder, lightning and rain; the heavenly constellations; the wild animals that live and breed out of the sight of human beings—all of these are under God's command, not ours.

A Greek philosopher of the fifth century BC, called Protagoras, said, 'Man is the measure of all things', but he was wrong.

One summer I travelled by rail from Paris to the south of France. Waiting on a station platform, I saw a man standing in the open doorway of a train. He was perfectly framed there, each hand resting comfortably on a side wall, his head not quite touching the archway above. It struck me that (yes, obviously!) we design and make trains human-sized, for human use, under human control.

When I arrived at the campsite where I was to stay for a fortnight, I found that it was situated above a river gorge. The cliffs I could see beside the river were not human-sized, designed and made for human use. The man I'd seen on the train, if standing against these sheer walls, would have been dwarfed, not framed, by them. At night-time in that place, the Milky Way was visible with a brightness of individual massed stars that I had never seen before. 'Have you comprehended the vast expanses of the earth?' God asks (Job 38:18). The answer has to be 'No.'

Will you have a chance, this summer, to go out and observe a part of the natural world that is not carefully managed for human use—the ocean, the mountains or the desert? Perhaps you'll be privileged enough to look down on vast expanses of sea or inhospitable land masses from the window of an aeroplane.

The natural response to such sights is a feeling of awe—and it may be a mistake to try to give your own creative expression to it. Even taking a photo may be an attempt to cut the experience down to size, putting a boundary around something that in reality is too big to fit within any human framework. Perhaps the only proper response is to worship the creator of it all.

As you go out today, look for examples of God-sized creation, of his work done to his measurements.

Big worries, bigger God

Creative

God's wisdom as creator goes hand in hand with his wisdom and compassion as the provider for his creation. Psalm 104 focuses on this aspect of his lordship over the vast expanses of the earth. God provides for the basic needs of all the creatures he has made—water, food and shelter (vv. 10–18, 27–28).

Jesus picked up this theme in Matthew 6:25–34 when he told his disciples never to worry about the essentials of life: 'Look at the birds of the air... your heavenly Father feeds them' and 'See how the flowers of the field grow... not even Solomon in all his splendour was dressed like one of these.'

Sometimes our anxieties seem so much bigger than ourselves that they threaten to overwhelm us. It may sound trite, but it is nevertheless true, that the creator God is bigger than any of our problems. It is also true that the God who set the moon and stars in place cares about human beings, with all their turbulent emotions (Psalm 8:3–4).

Find a piece of paper, as large as possible. Make a rough drawing or a painting on it of one of the natural elements mentioned in Psalm 104—the heavens with moon and stars, the ocean, the mountains, a forest or simply an expanse of bright light. Then write a list, on the same paper, of the things you're worried about at the moment, big and small. Finally, pray over each item on the list, entrusting it to the world's creator and provider.

Seeds of wisdom

Reflective

Let's go back to Genesis 1. On the third day of creation, in verses 11–12, vegetation appears, and the writer tells us not just that there are plants and trees but that the plants are 'seed-bearing' and the trees 'bear fruit with seed in it, according to their various kinds'.

What an astonishing idea a seed is! It's a powerhouse in miniature, containing all the energy necessary to grow and develop into an adult form that bears no resemblance to its starting point. Whether we're thinking of a flower seed, a tree fruit such as a sycamore key, a stone from a plum or cherry, or even the sperm and egg that produce a new human or other mammal, the shape and colour of the fully grown plant or animal that will emerge from that tiny seed is unimaginable. Just as amazing is that the adult form then produces more of the seeds, and so the process of reproduction continues.

In God's creative wisdom, greatness comes from small beginnings, and small size does not equal insignificance. In our culture, overcrowded with images and noise, with aggressive advertising campaigns promoting the latest big thing, all competing for the most 'clicks' and 'likes', we can be given the impression that only the spectacular is worth noticing. Even so, we do still know the proverbs that say 'The longest journey starts with a single step' and 'From little acorns giant oaks grow'. Many of us will remember, too, in the film *Star Wars: The Empire Strikes Back*, that the tiny Jedi Master Yoda says to Luke Skywalker indignantly, 'Judge me by my size, do you?' The wisdom of God in the creation of seeds is still recognised as a guiding principle in the judgement of what really matters.

As Zechariah 4:10 says, 'Who dares despise the day of small things…?'

Seeds of inspiration

Creative

The 14th-century mystic Julian of Norwich famously saw a vision of a hazelnut. Marvelling at its fragility and small size, she asked, 'What may this be?' and received an answer from God: 'It is all that is made… It lasts and ever shall, for God loves it, and so everything has its beginning by the love of God' (*Revelations of Divine Love*, c. 1393, ch. 5).

Cut a piece of fruit in half and take out the pips or stone. Spend some time meditating on the potential for explosive growth that is held within a single seed. There are many directions in which your thoughts might wander from this starting point. Jesus used seeds as a picture of the word of God taking root and producing a harvest in the world (Luke 8:1–15), and Paul used them to explain the mystery of resurrection (1 Corinthians 15:35–44). Galatians 3:29 talks of Abraham's 'seed', meaning his descendants through Jesus Christ: the promise of salvation moves from generation to generation.

You might think in simple, earthly terms of the way a small act of kindness can send widening ripples of joy from one person to another. Perhaps you've received a seed of inspiration from someone else's words or actions that you could take further, and see it blossom later in your own work.

What else will you notice today that speaks of the extraordinary growth that can come from small beginnings? Let it lead you into thanksgiving and prayer. Ask God how you or your work could act as a seed in other people's lives, perhaps sending blessing from one generation to another.

Searching out wisdom

Reflective

Wisdom, according to Proverbs, is a loudmouth, shouting in the street. She yells out her advice from high places and in public spaces where crowds of people gather (1:20–21; 8:1–3). Paul believed, too, that God speaks unmistakably through his creation: 'Since the creation of the world God's invisible qualities—his eternal power and divine nature—have been clearly seen, being understood from what has been made' (Romans 1:20). God's wisdom is broadcast through the created world, as if through a public address system.

Here, though, is one of those paradoxes found often in the Bible, where two opposite things are equally true, because in Job 28 we find a beautiful poem about searching for God's wisdom in the hidden parts of his creation. Precious stones and metals are locked away in the rocks far underground, out of the sight of birds, wild animals and most human beings. Miners are the only people who 'lay bare the roots of the mountains… tunnel through the rock… [and] see all its treasures' (vv. 9–10).

Perhaps some aspects of God's wisdom, then, are not picked easily off the surface of life; instead we have to search for them in dark and difficult circumstances, like miners in a cave. This is hard work, needing courage and determination.

Proverbs 25:2 says, 'It is the glory of God to conceal a matter; to search out a matter is the glory of kings.' This is a proverb of King Solomon, whose God-given wisdom led him to explore many branches of academic study. 'He spoke about plant life, from the cedar of Lebanon to the hyssop that grows out of walls. He also spoke about animals and birds, reptiles and fish' (1 Kings 4:33).

'To search out a matter is the glory of kings.' Leaders in medical research seek out antidotes to disease that might be hidden in plant life. Meanwhile, leaders in science and technology search for hidden truths about the workings of our universe and about the resources we need to sustain our lives on earth. These 'kings' are engaged in a glorious occupation, according to Solomon.

Praying for the researchers

Intercession

Read through a newspaper or browse the internet for stories of people engaged in research, in any field of study that interests you. Perhaps you yourself are a researcher of some kind in your daily work, or perhaps friends or family members have this occupation.

Spend some time praying for the people and issues that catch your attention. In your intercession, bring all your thanksgiving and requests to God. Here are some suggestions to guide your prayers:

- Is there a medical issue that's close to your heart because of a personal connection?
- Is there an issue that you think requires more research than is currently being done?
- Think of the moral dilemmas that are sometimes faced by researchers.
- Pray for discoveries that could benefit poorer countries as well as our own.
- Ask for wise decisions to be made about which research projects should be funded and which should not.
- Is there something practical you can do to support a research project that has captured your imagination?

Mixtures

Creative

Countless new discoveries have been made in the centuries since the biblical writers of Wisdom literature were expressing their joy and wonder about the created world. We now know, for example, that the measurements made by our builder/architect God are so exact that life on our planet could not have appeared or been sustained if they had been adrift by the slightest margin. We also know something that the biblical writers don't seem even to hint at—that the astounding variety in creation all around us stems from an extremely limited stock of ingredients. All the 'ordinary matter' in the universe is made from just 118 elements (as far as we know), which combine to produce everything we see. Just as great trees grow from the powerhouse of a small seed, so enormous complexity comes from relative simplicity.

Some of these combinations are simply stunning: which of us could imagine that two invisible gases, hydrogen and oxygen, would bond to produce something so completely 'other' as liquid water—different to see, hear, touch and taste?

Made in the image of God, we base many of our artistic and scientific creations on beautiful mixtures of elements. The perfumer blends aromas; the cook or wine expert mixes flavours; the engineer combines physical materials. Without them, we wouldn't have the classic scent accord of rose and jasmine, the delicious cocktail of champagne and cassis, or carbon-ceramic brakes. Painters, of course, mix colours. I remember an older child in my Reception class snatching my latest unimaginative picture of a house and garden and showing me how to create pink flowers by merging red and white wax crayon. I was amazed and delighted, though a little upset that I hadn't been able to make this discovery for myself.

Print out a colour wheel from the internet, showing the three primary colours and the secondary colours that can be created by mixing them. Alternatively, if you have paints or crayons to hand, make one for yourself. Place it somewhere to remind you of God's creative combinations. Be especially aware today, whatever you see, hear, smell or taste, of the amazing wisdom of God in providing so much potential for beauty and usefulness through the blending of just a few elements.

Wisdom concealed

Creative

'To search out a matter is the glory of kings,' says Proverbs 25:2. As we've seen, though, that verse begins, 'It is the glory of God to conceal a matter.' The poem in Job 28 talks of the precious gems and metals hidden in the rocks, there to be mined by those with the courage and skill to dig them out—but it goes on (in vv. 12–28) to say that God's wisdom can't be pinned down even in these fabulous places. Like so many of the most precious things in life— love, peace, hope or faith—wisdom is not an object that can be seen or touched. We can only see or feel its effects. Yet it is of far greater value than jewels or gold, concealed from every living thing and 'only a rumour' in the ears of Death. God is the only one who 'knows where it dwells' (v. 23).

Although we know far more about God's wisdom in creation than the biblical writers could have imagined, the answers we find lead on to more and more questions. Some of those questions, however much we discover, will never be answered. However hard we search in the world we inhabit, we will grasp only so much of it, because some things are kept for his knowledge alone. 'It is the glory of God to conceal a matter,' and God guards his own glory jealously (Isaiah 42:8).

The wisdom of God in creation

How would you describe wisdom? Where have you seen or felt its effects in your own experience? Where have you caught glimpses of it in places you've never been to—perhaps places you've seen on the television, in films or on the internet? If you had to explain it to a visitor to our planet, what would you say? Write or draw or use another favourite art form to express your ideas.

Conclusion

Liturgy

Creator God,
You measured off the limits of the heavens and the earth
with wisdom rejoicing at your side.

You sculpted man and woman in your creative image
with wisdom rejoicing at your side.

You packed the blueprint of a tree into the body of a seed
with wisdom rejoicing at your side.

You bonded the elements and mixed the colours of light
with wisdom rejoicing at your side.

Open our eyes and our hearts
to delight in the wonderful wisdom of your creation,
and help us to trust you with the parts of it that you keep hidden
for the sake of your glory.
Amen

21 AUGUST–3 SEPTEMBER

Listening

Liz Hoare

Introduction

There is a constant refrain through scripture urging us to hear God's words and respond to them, to listen in order to live. There are words of promise from Genesis to Revelation, words of command, words of revelation, words of faith. The world we live in today is full of words and we are bombarded with a cacophony of sound. It is difficult to know which words we can trust, and many of us have learned to tune out simply to survive. Is it possible that we are missing some of the vital words of life that God is speaking in his desire to attract our attention? How may we learn to tune in to God's words so that we may hear them clearly? Then we will know for sure that 'It is the Lord' (as Eli tells Samuel in 1 Samuel 3:18).

We learn, very early on, the voices of those who we know offer us security and reassurance. We can hear them above the many other sounds that fill the air and we seek them out for refuge. The Bible urges us to hear God's voice: 'O that today you would listen to his voice!' (Psalm 95:7b, NRSV), and we see from the previous sentence in the psalm that this command is related to the image of God the shepherd and us his sheep. Jesus used the same image to describe his relationship with his followers in John 10:1–4. Sheep learn to hear the voice of the shepherd through experience. Jesus said, 'The gatekeeper opens the gate… and the sheep hear his voice. He calls his own sheep by name and leads them out' (John 10:3, NRSV). Listening to God's voice is all about developing a relationship with him. It takes practice, and that is the aim of this theme of 'Listening'.

How do we hear?

Bible reading

Read Genesis 12:1–9.

How did Abram know that it was God telling him to leave his country and his kindred and set out for a land that God would show him? He may have heard an audible voice or he may have understood an inner movement of his spirit that propelled him to trust and depart. How should we expect to hear God speaking to us? It seems as though God's command came to Abram out of the blue. Have you ever had such an experience? How may we know with the kind of confidence that can say 'It is the Lord'? The letter to the Hebrews reminds us that God's chief means of communicating to us now is through his Son, Jesus Christ, who dwells in us by his Holy Spirit. Truly, God is closer to us than our own breath, but how do we hear his voice? God's word is communicated to us in the Bible where we meet the Lord Jesus, the living Word. Asking God to speak to us, we begin to read prayerfully and with open ears so that we meditate on the scriptures and make connections with our own lives. David Foster, in *Reading with God* (Continuum, 2005), suggests that the best way to tune in to God speaking to us is to read as if Jesus himself is reading the scriptures to us. The first lesson of listening to the Bible in this way is to remember that it is God's agenda that is the point of the activity.

Read John 10:1–6 as if Jesus were reading it to you. You might find it helpful to read the passage aloud.

Listening to God in the Bible

Spotlight

Despite the truth that the Holy Spirit dwells in every believer, we

Listening

need one another to help us to listen to him. There are two key principles involved in listening to God. The first is that he will never contradict himself as he is revealed in the Bible. If we think we have heard God telling us something that is directly opposed to what the Bible says, we may be sure we have not heard correctly. The second principle, which is perhaps more difficult to follow in our individualistic culture, is that we need to check out with others what we think God is saying. We forget that the Bible is the book of a community and that both the Old and New Testaments were written and heard in community. When Paul addresses 'you' in his letters, it is almost always 'you' plural.

Spiritual direction is a ministry that many people have found life-giving because it involves being listened to closely and prayerfully by another and also both individuals listening to God together, seeking to discern his voice. We can learn from this for our everyday conversations so that we listen to more than simply the words of another and thus pray for and relate to one another better. Try meeting up with a friend and practise listening to each other talk about what is going on for you. Notice the body language as well as the words; notice what is not said, the pauses and the hints rather than direct speech. Notice the imagery used to aid description or explanation. Remember that Jesus is present and listening with you. End by praying for one another. It's a good idea to reflect back to each other what the experience both of listening and being listened to felt like. If listening to another person is not possible just now, try listening to a radio interview or programme such as *Desert Island Discs* and notice how the interviewer and interviewee interact.

Where do you listen to God's word in the company of others? Continue tuning in to God's voice by reading a Bible passage aloud, as if Jesus were reading it to you. You could use Isaiah 44:1–5; Isaiah 42:5–9; John 14:1–4; John 15:1–17 or a favourite passage.

Speak, Lord, for your servant is listening

Imaginative

Read 1 Samuel 3:1—4:1.

In this beautiful story we are told that 'the word of the Lord was rare in those days' (v. 1, NRSV). People, it seemed, had stopped listening and their ears were no longer attuned to God. This may have been why it took Eli so long to realise that Samuel was hearing God's voice. But there is a gentle allusion to hope when we are told that 'the lamp of the Lord had not yet gone out' (v. 3, NRSV).

The child Samuel slept, but his readiness to respond in obedience meant that he quickly grew alert and answered the call of his name. Three times he ran to Eli and three times was sent back. He hadn't yet learned to recognise God's voice, but his obedience to Eli helped his heart to be ready.

Play this story out in your imagination, allowing a picture of Samuel in the dimly lit temple lying down to sleep some distance from his master. Hear the voice, as yet unknown but calling your name, and notice how you react.

The story does not have a happy ending, for Samuel had hard words to report to Eli. Does the fear of what you might hear prevent you from being attuned to God's voice? Eli's wise response enabled Samuel to speak God's words and hide nothing (v. 18). This was a vital step in the growth to maturity and wisdom that was preparing Samuel to be used by God as prophet and leader. Samuel learned to trust God and grow.

Learning to listen

Going out

When Samuel prayed 'Speak, Lord, for your servant is listening', he had already been on a steep learning curve in how to listen. At first he did not recognise it was the Lord who was speaking to him. The same may be true of us, for we all have to learn to distinguish the voices we need to hear from the general buzz of sounds around us. Think of the last time you found yourself in a crowded place, perhaps a café or restaurant or as a spectator at a sporting event. In such situations we have to strain to hear what is being said to us and it helps enormously if we know the voice of the one we are trying to listen to. It is the same with the word of God: we have to learn to distinguish the voice of the Lord from other 'voices' that seek our attention.

Listening is a skill and, like all skills, it can improve with practice. I am writing this with a window open nearby. Outside there are various sounds and if I pause to listen I can begin to pick out what they are. There is the distant drone of a motorway, a sound I have become so accustomed to that I do not hear it any more, not least because I don't wish to do so! Closer to home is a lawnmower, and if I dwell on that sound it seems to loom larger than if I concentrate on other sounds. The sound I really like is the birdsong. If I listen carefully I can distinguish different kinds of birds. I am not very good at this but it's something I would like to get better at, so every now and then I pause and deliberately pay attention to naming individual birds: blackbird, sparrow, robin, chaffinch, and far away the mewing of a red kite.

Learning to listen to the sounds of nature is one way to practise honing our listening skills so that we become better at listening to one another and also make better connections between our world and the world of the Bible. In the days before mechanised sound, the writers of the Bible relied on imagery from the natural world to describe characteristics of God. These images instilled not only a sense of awe, like the roaring of the waters (Revelation 14:2), but also intimacy: the gentle breathing of a weaned child in its mother's arms (Psalm 131:2). When the Holy Spirit came in power at Pentecost, the disciples heard a sound 'like the rush of a violent wind' (Acts 2:2, NRSV). What sounds speak to you of the characteristics of God?

Go outside for a walk today, or sit near an open window, and listen to the sounds around you. If you live in a city, you will still be able to distinguish one sound from another. Do any of the sounds you hear lead you to think about an attribute of God or compel you to pray for something or someone as you listen?

The art of sacred reading

Meditative

In the Gospels Jesus speaks in many different ways. He called people to follow him, he told them stories, he taught them with authority, he uttered words of compassion and healing. People heard 'gladly', we are told. Today we have many of his words written down for us. Learning to hear God through the words of scripture, to listen to them as though they are addressed directly to us, is a joyful experience, for they offer us a way into the presence of the God who loves us and who longs to make his presence known to us daily. One age-old way of learning to listen to God in scripture is through the practice of *lectio divina*—the art of sacred reading. It helps us to slow down, to savour the words of the Bible and to hear God speaking to us. Our response in prayer is our side of the conversation: us speaking to God. And so through this dialogue our friendship with God may grow deeper and fill our whole lives, rather than being kept for set times of prayer.

Choose a favourite Bible story and read it aloud. This action alone will slow down the process of hearing so that we may listen carefully. Next, read it again slowly and prayerfully, allowing it to sink from the mind into the heart. How do we know when this has happened?

The process is different from a Bible study where we are reading to understand the structure and meaning of the text in its context. We can help the process of *lectio* by reading reflectively, listening for echoes, allusions to other parts of the Bible we are familiar with, experiences in our own lives which resonate with the words here, areas of life where we feel addressed by the passage and so on. We can also experience the passage becoming part of us as we repeat a phrase slowly, inwardly. It is a good idea to end the time with a prayer thanking God for what we have heard. It is surprising how often we will 'hear' a word or phrase from our reading echoing in our hearts during the coming day.

Here are some passages to try: John 14:23–26; 1 John 1:1–4; Deuteronomy 6:4–9; Psalm 121.

Listening to each other

Reflective

Our prayers for one another would be so much more focused if we listened more carefully to what people are saying and not saying. Radio 4 has a series of short conversations between two people called *The Listening Project*, and it is an invitation to listen in for a few minutes to two people who are listening to each other as well as talking. It is a breath of fresh air in a world overloaded with sound bites of people talking over one another or past each other with little effort to really hear what is being said. In the Gospels, Jesus frequently addressed large crowds and, as in the parable of the sower, he knew that some seed would immediately be snatched away, some would fall on stony ground and some would be choked by weeds later on. He often ended his addresses with the words 'Let anyone with ears to hear listen' (for example Mark 4:9, NRSV), knowing that many would go away and forget. The Gospels also show us conversations where lives are changed as a result of someone hearing Jesus address them personally. He seemed to know what lay behind the words being spoken. The encounter with the woman of Samaria in John 4 is one example of Jesus listening to the woman carefully and responding to her real, as opposed to her presenting, needs.

Read John 4 and focus on how Jesus invites, listens and leads the conversation with the woman. What do you notice? Try to follow his example in your conversations today.

Prayer

Father, I want to be a better listener. Please help me to listen to others as you listen.
Amen

Listening to the world

Intercession

Sometimes we assume we know what is needed, so we don't bother to stop and listen before launching in with our own plans and projects. The problem is that we may find ourselves answering questions no one is asking or performing actions that are futile or miss the mark. One thing we can do to help us be aware of what God is doing in the world is to learn to listen to it. If this sounds too big a task, we can break it down and begin by listening to our local community. What is in the air? What concerns do people have about life where we are?

From there, we can widen our horizons to read about what is happening in the wider world and what God is saying through events. When John Stott wrote about the issues that face Christians in the modern world, he described a biblical framework to help people think about them from a Christian perspective. The framework had four key points: Creation, Fall, Redemption and New Creation. Each of these helps us think biblically about what we see and hear around us. Creation speaks of God's basic values, the Fall shows us the reason why things have gone so wrong, Redemption encourages us that God has come into the mess and acted on our behalf, while the New Creation reminds us that this is not the end of the story.

What is in the news at the moment? Does it sound like redemption or remind us of the new creation that we hope for? We should also remember that this task is not best done in isolation. Churches can help people listen together so that they can respond more effectively. We can bring our concerns into the intercessory prayers of the church and we can consider whether God is asking us to do something.

Listen carefully to the news today and pray with the help of this biblical framework. Talk to others in your church to see how you could pray together and listen to what God is saying to you as his body.

Listening to the world

Intercession/creative

A young couple go to live on a new housing estate. For a year they simply live there and get to know the neighbours, eventually opening their home and offering hospitality, especially at Christmas, Easter and other special times. Slowly a community is built, and because the couple make no secret of the fact they love Jesus they are able to speak of what he means to them and invite others to consider his claims for themselves. Mission starts with listening. If we fail to listen, we will find ourselves offering answers to questions people are not asking, we will try to impose our way of doing things on people who cannot relate to us in that way.

As we learn to listen to God, we discover that we are also learning to listen to his world more and to listen to it from his perspective. Someone has said that 'whoever lays their head on the breast of Jesus hears the heartbeat of God'. Since God 'so loved the world', we should expect our own love for it to grow.

There are many ways we can listen better to the world around us so that we may pray, live and join in with what God is doing. Spending times apart with God to listen to him is of primary importance. To practise listening to the world, try listening to what concerns people who live near you or who work with you, and take their concerns to God in prayer. Jot down some news items from whatever media you normally use and write a letter to God about them.

Learning to listen with God

Reflective

Read Isaiah 50:4–5.

This passage is one of the so-called 'Servant songs' which point forwards to Christ as well as speaking to the prophet's contemporaries. There are some key principles in the way the prophet listened to God that may help us learn to listen with the ear of an attentive disciple today.

First, it is God who takes the initiative here: 'The Lord has given me the tongue of a teacher' (NRSV). When we feel an inner impulse to speak to someone in Christ's name (a word of comfort to the weary), this is where our confidence lies. Another point to notice is that learning to listen doesn't happen instantaneously but over time, 'morning by morning'. Furthermore, God works with us in partnership, not overruling who we are. He 'opens our ear', but it is up to us to stay and listen. Here the prophet has not turned away or resisted but chosen to listen, even in the face of difficult consequences. There may be a cost in listening well which may come our way, though others may be blessed.

Are you aware of any cost in making yourself available to listen to God and to others? Speak to the Lord about it in the quiet now.

It may be that you have found the cost of not being heard yourself a painful reality and built up resistance to listening in return as a way of dealing with the pain. Think of situations where you find it difficult to listen and bring them to Christ in prayer, asking him to heal and restore your ability to hear and respond.

Choices

Reflective

*'Incline your ear, and come to me;
listen, so that you may live.'*
ISAIAH 55:3, NRSV

This verse suggests that listening is a matter of life and death, vital for the health and well-being of the human soul.

What is your favourite sound? It's a fascinating question and reveals all kinds of evocative answers: birdsong, the waves of the sea lapping the shore, a solo saxophone playing a haunting tune. For the young woman in the Song of Songs it was the voice of the beloved: 'The voice of my beloved! Look, he comes, leaping upon the mountains, bounding over the hills' (Song of Songs 2:8). She heard his voice before she saw him and it thrilled her and filled her with delight and anticipation. Her desire for her beloved kept her alert and listening.

In chapter 5 she is asleep yet her heart is alert, listening for the knock of the beloved at the door, even as she slumbers (5:2). This is akin to praying without ceasing. It suggests an attitude of receptivity to God's voice, a stance of awareness that does not tune out the airwaves, even when doing something else. It is the reverse of the famous poem 'The Listeners' by Walter de la Mare, which begins:

> *'Is there anybody there?' said the Traveller,*
> *Knocking on the moonlit door...*

He knocked but no one came, no one responded. There was no one at home, save the ghosts of former occupants, and the traveller went away disappointed. In the familiar picture by Holman Hunt, *The Light of the World*, it is Jesus himself standing outside the door with a lantern in his hand, knocking and seeking entrance. There is no handle on the outside of the door, so he is dependent on the person inside hearing and opening up to welcome him in. Hunt was painting the image of Christ in Revelation 3:20: 'Listen! I am standing at the door, knocking; if you hear my voice and open the door, I will come in to you and eat with you, and you with me' (NRSV). It is an invitation from the Lord himself to make his home in us.

Listening and stillness

Reflective

One of the most basic helps in learning to listen is to find somewhere quiet where other noise does not interfere. Jesus was in the habit of getting up early and going off to a lonely place to pray (Mark 1:35). Most of us will have to be very intentional about finding quiet places to pray because our culture immerses us in noise. We have to learn to be quiet and to listen to the quiet.

One of the ways the early Celtic Christians continue to inspire Christians today is the way they knew when to be alone with God and when to engage with the world. They sought time alone

Listening

for prayer, often in remote places, but they practised living in community too, surrounding the whole of life with prayer. They were conscious of God in everything and made no distinction between sacred and secular. Perhaps it was this openness to the wind of God's Spirit that made the early Celtic Christians such effective evangelists. They did not devise elaborate programmes or strategies for evangelism, but went (often walking or sailing their coracles) as wanderers for Christ's sake, sharing the good news with whoever would listen. They knew that God was already there before them, at work in his world, and they were being invited to join in. Most of us find it difficult to get away to be alone with God in order to listen to him. Find some time this week when you can press 'pause' and 'Be still, and know that [he is] God' (Psalm 46:10).

On holiday with God

Sally Smith

It's the holiday season again and many of you will be going away for a few days, or for a longer period. Some people see holidays as a time to have a break from the busyness of their local church and from regular commitments. For others it is a time to visit other churches and see what is happening in the wider Christian world; to meet Christians from other backgrounds and learn what God is doing in other places. Hopefully for all of us it is a time to slow down and see the world differently. Part of this seeing differently can be in making a conscious effort to find God in the places we visit and the time we have available. If you are 'holidaying at home', there is no reason not to try out some of the ideas here as you endeavour to slow down and relax.

There are many ways in which you could try and spend some time with God when you are away. You might want to find a special place where you can go and spend some time each day; this may well be outside—a garden or somewhere with an amazing view—or it may be a quiet space indoors where you know you won't be disturbed. Try and make a routine of visiting that place each day that you are away, acknowledging God's presence as you arrive and settle there.

Or, if you establish a daily routine while you are away, you might like to try and build in a specific period each day when you set aside time to be with God. You might find it then translates into your daily routine back at home, but while you are away and may have slightly more energy and time, it's a good opportunity to try things out and see what might work for you.

If you are travelling around a lot, you might prefer to commit to visiting at least one church every day and sitting in silence in the building or the churchyard for half an hour. You could commit to visiting every church you pass, but you may find you end up spending all your holiday in churches, so be realistic in anything you commit yourself to.

Consciously invite God to travel with you. This can be a prayer at the beginning of each day, or a continuous conversation with him about what is happening, both what you can see and what is going on within you. Obviously it makes a difference whether you are travelling alone or with others! You could imagine God in the seat next to you; conscious of his presence, I find this makes me a much better driver as I carry such a precious passenger.

Use what is around you—use all your senses and be aware of your surroundings. Spend time acknowledging what is there and thanking God for his amazing creation. You might get caught up in the rhythm of the waves on the sea, or the variety of his creation as you sit outside enjoying a coffee.

You might collect resources as you travel that you can take back home to use in your prayer time over the coming year. These could be postcards and pictures from art galleries, natural items, locally made products, or pictures and leaflets you pick up.

If you are travelling some distance, the journey can become tiresome, so why not set a challenge of reading a Christian book that's been sitting on the pile for a while, or practise being still in God's presence? Or you could read a spiritual book slowly over the holiday, stopping each time a sentence catches your attention, spending time with those words before moving on. You may not finish your book, but you may grow through the process.

It can be helpful to keep a journal with you on holiday, using it to record all that God gives to you while you are away: noting the gifts he gives and the times and places where you have met him. Alternatively, you could take photos of those 'God moments' and save them in a separate file to reflect on and offer thanks for, either later in the day or when you get home.

If you don't already do so, you could try reflecting at the end of each day on where you have met with God and what he has given you. This is another helpful habit that might transfer back to ordinary life.

Remember, you are on holiday, not on retreat; they are different and have different purposes. So, whatever you are doing, and however you choose to include God in your plans, may your holiday be all you wish it to be and may you meet with God along the way.

As a Child

Phil Steer

Obedient

> *As* obedient *children, do not conform to the evil desires you had when you lived in ignorance.*
> 1 PETER 1:14, NIV 1984, emphasis mine

When my daughter turned eleven she received a birthday card that proclaimed, '"Getting older is fun, it means you don't have to do what you're told" (Molly, aged six)'. This young child's remark makes us smile because, even as grown-ups, we recognise the truth of it. For children are forever being told what to do, forever having their lives ordered by others. From when to get up to when to go to bed, and all points in between: eat this food, wear these clothes, go to school, do this work, come here, go there, do this, don't do that, and so on and so on. Of course, as adults our days are far from wholly our own but, nonetheless, most of us would struggle to cope with even a fraction of the commands and demands that children are expected to follow, with their lack of autonomy and self-determination.

Perhaps this is why some of us struggle with the whole concept—still more the practice—of obedience to God. Instinctively we agree with Molly: we're grown-ups now and old enough to decide for ourselves how we live our lives. We don't need or want anyone else—even God—telling us what to do.

Little children need to be told what to do because they do not yet have the experience and maturity to make wise and appropriate decisions for themselves. They need looking after and they need a strong guiding hand. And in some ways this is true of us as children of God. Our heavenly Father knows far better than we do how we should live our lives, and he wants to protect us from situations and behaviour that would be damaging to ourselves or to others. It is in our very best interests to open our ears to his instructions and commands—through his word, through the words of others, through the prompting of his Holy Spirit, through whatever means he chooses—and to respond with the obedience of little children.

But in seeking obedience from our children, those of us who are parents are doing more than trying to ensure that they do the right thing here and now, in this or that situation. More importantly, we are trying to prepare them for the future, to teach them how to behave, to know 'right from wrong,' to be able to make those wise and appropriate decisions for themselves. As the book of Proverbs counsels, 'Train a child in the way he should go, and when he is old he will not turn from it' (Proverbs 22:6). We seek to train our children in obedience in the hope that they will choose to walk in obedience.

For true obedience is to be found, not so much in doing as we are told, as in doing for ourselves what we already know to be right. As Paul wrote to the church in Ephesus, 'Slaves, obey your earthly masters... not only to win their favour when their eye is on you, but like slaves of Christ, doing the will of God from your heart' (Ephesians 6:5–6). If this is how it was to be between slaves and their masters, how much more should it be between children and their parents, and between children of God and their heavenly Father.

As parents, we don't want forever to be telling our children what to do and when to do it, to be making all their decisions for them. Rather, we want them more and more to take responsibility for themselves, to make their own way in the world, to flourish and to grow as the individuals that God has created them to be. Yes, we will always be there for them, ready to offer our advice and counsel if it is needed and asked for, but we will no longer be directing and determining their lives as we once did. And this is how it should be.

In the same way, I believe, God does not want us to become mindlessly dependent on him, forever asking him what to do, never making any decisions ourselves, never taking any responsibility ourselves. Rather, as our perfect parent, he wants us to grow in our faith, to be 'trained in obedience', so that increasingly we will know and choose for ourselves 'the way we should go'. As Paul wrote to the church in Rome, 'Be transformed by the renewing of your mind. Then you will be able to test and approve what God's will is—his good, pleasing and perfect will' (Romans 12:2).

In the book of Deuteronomy we find the following promise and encouragement from God to his people, 'Now what I am commanding you today is not too difficult for you or beyond your reach… No, the word is very near you; it is in your mouth and in your heart so that you may obey it' (Deuteronomy 30:11, 14). God has told us how to live through his commandments. He has placed this word in our heart by his Holy Spirit. Now we are not to sit wondering and worrying about what to do, but rather to set off to walk in obedience, trusting that he will be there at our shoulder to help us stay on the straight and narrow. 'Whether you turn to the right or to the left, your ears will hear a voice behind you, saying, "This is the way; walk in it"' (Isaiah 30:21).

Jesus said that he had come that we might have life in all its fullness (John 10:10); yet, as a friend so astutely observed, too often Christianity looks more like life in all its emptiness. Like children over-anxious to please their parents, we can be paralysed into inaction; so desperate to do right (or not do wrong) that we do nothing. But God, I believe, is far more frustrated by our inaction than he is by the mistakes that we make in trying to live our lives.

Jesus came and lived and died to enable us to live and make mistakes. Not that we should deliberately sin, or put ourselves into the path of temptation ('By no means!' says Paul in Romans

6:1–2). But were there no forgiveness in and through Jesus, we would indeed be paralysed by the fear of doing wrong—although our inaction would, of course, be sin itself ('in the evil we have done and the good we have not done', Alternative Confession A, Order for Holy Communion Rite A, *The Alternative Service Book 1980*). But because of Jesus we can go out into the world and live, seeking to bring his life and light into the deadness and darkness, risking failure and mistakes, because we know that he will not condemn us, but rather forgive us, restore us and set us right.

Of course, there are times when God wants us to obey not just his universal commands to all people, but also his specific direction for us as individuals—and I know that I for one have a long way to go when it comes to learning to listen and being willing to obey. I must admit to having a certain fondness for Jonah who, when God told him, 'Go to the great city of Nineveh and preach against it,' instead 'ran away from the Lord and headed for Tarshish' (Jonah 1:2–3). I strongly suspect that I would have done the same.

But the more we learn to be obedient to God's universal commands, the more we will be prepared to obey when he gives us specific direction. And this may even have been true of Jesus: for the writer of the book of Hebrews tells us, 'Although he was a son, he learned obedience from what he suffered' (Hebrews 5:8).

At first sight this would seem to suggest that before Jesus 'learned obedience' he must have been disobedient. But this cannot be right because the same writer tells us that Jesus was 'tempted in every way, just as we are—yet was without sin' (Hebrews 4:15). So it is not that Jesus was ever disobedient, but rather that his obedience reached new levels in his suffering and death on the cross. The self-denial and self-sacrifice that was asked of him by his heavenly Father was more than had ever been asked of him before; was more indeed, than had ever, or would ever, be asked of anyone in the history of the world.

At his moment of decision in the Garden of Gethsemane Jesus

knew that he faced the prospect of an agonising death nailed to a cross. Yet this was not what made his obedience unique, for countless others have suffered similarly horrible deaths. No, terrible as this was, Jesus faced something far more terrible still: to have all the sins of the world piled upon him—as if it were he who had thought and said and done all of these things—and so to lose the intimacy that he had enjoyed with his Father from everlasting to everlasting.

This was no easy thing, even for the Son of God. As Luke tells us, 'Being in anguish, he prayed more earnestly, and his sweat was like drops of blood falling to the ground' (Luke 22:44). And it was at this point, when his Father was asking him to make the ultimate sacrifice, that Jesus demonstrated his ultimate obedience: 'Father, if you are willing, take this cup from me; yet not my will, but yours be done' (Luke 22:42).

Could it be that even Jesus had to be brought to this level of obedience? That if the cross had come earlier in his life and ministry he might at that time have been unable to go through with it? For we must always remember that, although fully God, Jesus was also fully human. He came as a baby and he needed to grow. He grew in strength (Luke 2:40) and he grew in wisdom (Luke 2:52), so why should he not also grow in obedience? And if Jesus grew into obedience to what God was calling him to do, then so can we.

Obedience requires the setting aside of self, and of self-determination—of the freedom to feel that we can have what we want and do what we want whenever we want. It requires, in a word, humility. 'Your attitude should be the same as that of Jesus Christ: Who... being found in appearance as a man... humbled himself and became obedient to death—even death on a cross!' (Philippians 2:5, 8).

The humility of Christ was the humility of a little child, for he 'made himself nothing' (Philippians 2:7), as a little child is 'nothing'. And the obedience of Christ was the obedience of a little child, for it came not from submission to authority like a slave with his master, but rather from the childlike relationship with his heavenly Father; for he did what he saw his Father doing (John 5:19). This was not primarily obedience to instruction and command, but rather a heartfelt desire to join his Father in his work. And as it was for Christ, so should it be for us.

Spotlight: The Greenhouse Christian Centre

Kate Strand

Sixty years ago, Sister Ruth Hainsworth felt led by God to set up a place that became known as Green Pastures Centre of Healing. And people came—sometimes in ambulances—broken, bruised, rejected, needing God's healing in their lives, and they were healed. They stayed for as long as they needed, gave what they could, worked out their healing as they recovered and eventually moved on to all that God had for them away from Green Pastures. The full story can be read in *Led to Green Pastures* by Ruth Hainsworth (Arthur James Ltd, 1977).

Like many retreat centres, we came to the point a few years ago where we nearly had to close. At that very painful time, God spoke clearly that he still had a plan and a purpose for this house. A new vision was given—that we would be a place where Christians could come to be **restored**, **equipped** and **connected**.

Restore—to be a place where people can rest, recover, be built up by immersing themselves in the Word and the Spirit, be nurtured, looked after, be safe.

Equip—to access teaching and resources so as to be more able to be 'useful' and effective in life and ministry.

Connect—to be a meeting place where Christians can come together, deepen relationships with the Lord and one another, and meet others who help them to grow in their faith and work.

Last year the final piece of this new vision was put into place—a new name! We all know that God is in the business of changing names—Jacob to Israel, Saul to Paul, Abram to Abraham, Simon to Peter—but it was never done on a whim; it was because he wanted to do a wonderful new work through them and establish them in a new identity.

We believe our new name—The Greenhouse Christian Centre—is the seal on this new identity.

I think it's fair to say that all of us find change challenging in one way or another. Below is a poem that one of our team has written about this change and the new season of work here. It is a wonderful illustration of the place we seek to be.

The Greenhouse

Come inside, out of the cold.
Rest a while,
Grow a little,
Find strength.
Be nurtured and well fed.
Let the sun warm you
In transparency and light.
Let the gardener tend you,
Let him add MiracleGro
If he wants to.
If he needs to.
Be around others,
Like you, but different.
Leave stronger,
Healthier,
More fruitful.
Be replanted,
Put down roots.

Spotlight: The Greenhouse Christian Centre

Sow,
And reap,
And live.

That's the offer for all of us. Will you take it up?

For more information, please call us on 01202 764776, www.the-greenhouse.org or email info@the-greenhouse.org

BRF Quiet Days

BRF Quiet Days are an ideal way of redressing the balance in our busy lives. Held in peaceful locations around the country, each one is led by an experienced speaker and gives the opportunity to reflect, be silent and pray, and, through it all, to draw closer to God.

Here is the programme for 2017:

Thursday 4 May: 'For My Safe: Paul's letter to Philemon' led by Bridget and Adrian Plass at Scargill House, Kettlewell, North Yorkshire BD23 5HU

Friday 16 June: 'St Francis and the Humanity of Jesus' led by David Walker at Bishopscourt, Bury New Road, Salford, Greater Manchester M7 4LE

Monday 19 June: 'The Contemplative Minister' led by Ian Cowley at Launde Abbey, East Norton, Leicestershire LE7 9XB

Monday 10 July: A teaching day on the theme of 'Attentive to God' led by Tony Horsfall at The Mirfield Centre, Stocks Bank Road, Mirfield, West Yorkshire WF14 0BW

Thursday 21 September: 'Living Deeply and Well in Later Life' led by Debbie Thrower at Old Alresford Place, Alresford, Hampshire SO24 9DH

Thursday 9 November: 'Marks upon the Heart: Pilgrim journeys, lessons for life' led by Sally Welch at The Carmelite Priory, Boars Hill, Oxford OX1 5HB

Friday 10 November: 'Hope in Unexpected Places' led by Ellie Hart at Shallowford House, Shallowford, Stone, Staffordshire ST15 0NZ

For further details and to book, please go to **brfonline.org.uk/events-and-quiet-days** or contact us at BRF, 15 The Chambers, Vineyard, Abingdon OX14 3FE; tel: +44 (0)1865 319700.

Finding God in all things, hearing God's voice for ourselves and others… the *Quiet Spaces Prayer Journal* will help you to develop and maintain a life of creative prayer. With space to write and quotations drawn from Christian tradition and from *Quiet Spaces* to aid reflection, this is ideal for you or as a gift for anyone wanting to deepen their prayer life.

Quiet Spaces Prayer Journal
ISBN 978 0 85746 524 5 £9.99

brfonline.org.uk

QUIET SPACES SUBSCRIPTION FORM

All our Bible reading notes can be ordered online by visiting biblereadingnotes.org.uk/subscriptions

If you and a minimum of **four** friends subscribe to *Quiet Spaces* or BRF's other Bible reading notes (*New Daylight*, *Day by Day with God*, *Guidelines*, *The Upper Room*), you can form a group. What's so good about being in a group? You pay the price of the notes only —postage is free for delivery to a UK address. (All notes are sent to one address.) All group orders are invoiced. No advance payment is required. For more information, see **biblereadingnotes.org.uk/group-subscriptions** or contact the BRF office.

Title .... First name/initials .... Surname ....

Address ....

.... Postcode ....

Telephone .... Email ....

INDIVIDUAL SUBSCRIPTION Please send *Quiet Spaces* beginning with the September 2017 / January 2018 / May 2018 issue (*delete as appropriate*):

	Quantity	UK	Europe	Rest of world
(per 3 issues)	☐	☐ £16.50	☐ £24.60	☐ £28.50

Total enclosed £ .... (cheques should be made payable to 'BRF')

Please charge my MasterCard / Visa ☐ Debit card ☐ with £ ....

Card no. ☐☐☐☐ ☐☐☐☐ ☐☐☐☐ ☐☐☐☐

Valid from M M Y Y   Expires M M Y Y   Security code* ☐☐☐
Last 3 digits on the reverse of the card

Signature* .... Date ....../....../......

*ESSENTIAL IN ORDER TO PROCESS YOUR ORDER

To set up a Direct Debit, please also complete the Direct Debit instruction on the reverse of this form.

GROUP SUBSCRIPTION (UK only) Please send *Quiet Spaces* beginning with the September 2017 / January 2018 / May 2018 issue (*delete as appropriate*):

Quantity ☐ (Current price per issue: £4.40)

Please invoice me: per issue / annually (*delete as appropriate*).

Please return this form to:
BRF, 15 The Chambers, Vineyard, Abingdon OX14 3FE
To read our terms and find out about cancelling your order, please visit **brfonline.org.uk/terms**.

The Bible Reading Fellowship is a Registered Charity (233280)

The Bible Reading Fellowship

Instruction to your bank or building society to pay by Direct Debit

DIRECT Debit

Please fill in the whole form using a ballpoint pen and return it to:
BRF, 15 The Chambers, Vineyard, Abingdon OX14 3FE

Service User Number: | 5 | 5 | 8 | 2 | 2 | 9 |

Name and full postal address of your bank or building society

To: The Manager	Bank/Building Society
Address	
	Postcode

Name(s) of account holder(s)

Branch sort code

Bank/Building Society account number

Reference number

Instruction to your Bank/Building Society
Please pay The Bible Reading Fellowship Direct Debits from the account detailed in this instruction, subject to the safeguards assured by the Direct Debit Guarantee. I understand that this instruction may remain with The Bible Reading Fellowship and, if so, details will be passed electronically to my bank/building society.

Signature(s)

Banks and Building Societies may not accept Direct Debit instructions for some types of account.

DIRECT DEBIT PAYMENT

You can pay for your annual subscription to our Bible reading notes using Direct Debit. You need only give your bank details once, and the payment is made automatically every year until you cancel it. If you would like to pay by Direct Debit, please use the form opposite, entering your BRF account number under 'Reference number'.

You are fully covered by the Direct Debit Guarantee:

The Direct Debit Guarantee

- This Guarantee is offered by all banks and building societies that accept instructions to pay Direct Debits.

- If there are any changes to the amount, date or frequency of your Direct Debit, The Bible Reading Fellowship will notify you 10 working days in advance of your account being debited or as otherwise agreed. If you request The Bible Reading Fellowship to collect a payment, confirmation of the amount and date will be given to you at the time of the request.

- If an error is made in the payment of your Direct Debit, by The Bible Reading Fellowship or your bank or building society, you are entitled to a full and immediate refund of the amount paid from your bank or building society.

- If you receive a refund you are not entitled to, you must pay it back when The Bible Reading Fellowship asks you to.

- You can cancel a Direct Debit at any time by simply contacting your bank or building society. Written confirmation may be required. Please also notify us.

This page is left blank for your notes.